The
Reference Shelf®

The News and Its Future

Edited by Paul McCaffrey

The Reference Shelf
Volume 82 • Number 2
The H.W. Wilson Company
New York • Dublin
2010

The Reference Shelf

The books in this series contain reprints of articles, excerpts from books, addresses on current issues, and studies of social trends in the United States and other countries. There are six separately bound numbers in each volume, all of which are usually published in the same calendar year. Numbers one through five are each devoted to a single subject, providing background information and discussion from various points of view and concluding with a subject index and comprehensive bibliography that lists books, pamphlets, and abstracts of additional articles on the subject. The final number of each volume is a collection of recent speeches, and it contains a cumulative speaker index. Books in the series may be purchased individually or on subscription.

Library of Congress has cataloged this serial title as follows:

The news and its future / edited by Paul McCaffrey.
      p. cm. — (The reference shelf ; v. 82, no. 2)
    Includes bibliographical references and index.
    ISBN 978-0-8242-1097-7 (alk. paper)
    1. Citizen journalism—United States. 2. Journalism--Technological innovations—United States. 3. Online journalism—United States. 4. Journalism—Objectivity—United States. I. McCaffrey, Paul, 1977–
    PN4784.C615N49 2010
    071'.3—dc22

                             2010005256

Cover: "Printing Press", James Hard/Getty Images

Visit H.W. Wilson's Web site: www.hwwilson.com

Printed in the United States of America

Contents

Preface

In 1997 the Committee of Concerned Journalists, a group affiliated with the Project for Excellence in Journalism (PEJ), began a four-year exploration to determine what principles ought to serve as the foundation of contemporary journalism. They settled on nine in total: 1. Journalism's first obligation is to the truth; 2. Its first loyalty is to citizens; 3. Its essence is a discipline of verification; 4. Its practitioners must maintain an independence from those they cover; 5. It must serve as an independent monitor of power; 6. It must provide a forum for public criticism and compromise; 7. It must strive to make the significant interesting and relevant; 8. It must keep the news comprehensive and proportional; 9. Its practitioners must be allowed to exercise their personal conscience.

As these principles were being laid out, however, forces were already at work to undermine their feasibility. More than that, these same forces were threatening the long-term viability of mainstream journalism as we know it. In the nearly ten years since these tenets were proposed, the journalistic landscape has been transformed. Technology, most obviously in the form of the Internet, has fundamentally revolutionized how news is gathered and consumed, leaving in its wake a trail of creative innovation and destruction. Many question whether the new journalism that is emerging is capable of shouldering the heavy responsibility required of a free press.

The selections gathered in this volume of The Reference Shelf consider the current state of the news media and the factors that are shaping its future. One of the central questions they seek to answer is how the new journalistic models compare to the old, and whether they are capable of living up to the high calling espoused in the nine principles of journalism put forth by the Committee of Concerned Journalists.

Not only has the Internet given the public access to countless news sources, allowing them to pick and choose their content from a near-infinite variety of material, it has furnished citizens with the tools to become journalists themselves. Anyone can now start a Web log, or blog, and comment on the day's events, or, better yet, report on them themselves. Given the increasing affordability of recording equipment, people can post more than just black and white text, but can contribute audio, videos, and other content to the Web as well. In other words, the barrier between the press and the public is disappearing. Articles in the first chapter, "The Democratization of the News: The Internet and the Rise of Citizen Journalism," consider this important trend. Indeed, of all the forces impacting the news media, none is perhaps more essential to understanding recent developments than the democratization process. In many respects, the technology-driven rise of citizen journalism is the engine propelling the current transformation of the news. Of course, this process is not a seamless one and has had a number of messy consequences.

A mainstay of journalism for hundreds of years, the newspaper has absorbed much of the impact of the Internet tidal wave. The damage inflicted on the newspaper's bottom line is considerable, leading to cutbacks in nearly all phases of the business. Some reputable publications have even gone under, leading many observers to write the industry's epitaph. Whether the newspaper will be able to navigate the shifting currents is an open question. Entries in the second chapter, "The Newspaper Crisis: Print Media in the Crosshairs," consider the recent fortunes of the newspaper industry and whether the future shows any promise for recovery.

Those who followed the 2008 presidential election no doubt heard charges of media bias hurled by one side or another. Not by any means are these accusations novel: people have been making them for generations. Nevertheless, with the rise of the Internet and the expansion of politically motivated content in print, on television, and on-line, such charges have grown louder and their side effects more pronounced. Convinced of the bias of mainstream media, consumers can now limit their news choices to only those sources that affirm their beliefs, tuning out any news that might conflict with their viewpoint. In "Media Bias: The Politics of Journalism," selections consider not only whether the news media has a political agenda, but what consequences the perception of media bias has on the public and how it informs itself.

Just as the Internet has reshaped the news industry, so too has the emergence of cable television, particularly cable news. Barely 20 years ago, the network newscasts were the public's main source of television news. In the United States, viewers could tune in to a half-hour of national news a night on one of the three major networks. With the emergence of CNN, MSNBC, and Fox News, however, that half an hour of news ballooned to 24 hours. The strengths and drawbacks of this system are the focus of articles in the final chapter, "The 24-Hour News Cycle: The Cable News Effect."

In conclusion, I would like to thank the many authors and publishers who granted permission to reprint their work in these pages. I would also like to thank the many friends and colleagues at the H.W. Wilson Company who helped in producing this volume, especially Joseph Miller, Carolyn Ellis, Kenneth Partridge, and Richard Stein.

Paul McCaffrey
April 2010

1

The Democratization of the News:
The Internet and the Rise of Citizen Journalism

Editor's Introduction

The news industry is in the midst of a period of profound transition. The advent of the Internet Age has rendered obsolete long-standing models of how to gather and communicate the news. What new paradigms will emerge to replace the old is unclear. Indeed, given the breakneck pace at which change has occurred over the past two decades, it's likely that we are in for an era of perpetual transformation, one with few certainties and no fixed outcome.

Yet there are some truths on which we can rely: technology will remain an agent of near constant change, and one of its major consequences will be an ongoing leveling of the barrier between the press and the public. This democratization of the news media can already be widely observed. All those with Internet access can now start their own Web log, or blog, posting their own news items, thoughts, music, videos, and analysis and transmitting them electronically throughout the globe. Using the social networking capabilities of the Internet, they can likewise interact with their readers, receive and respond to feedback, and otherwise engage in a continuing conversation.

The selections collected in this chapter perform two functions: they chart the democratization of the news media and speculate on what the ultimate implication of this trend will be. Already some are convinced that this process will lead to a dumbing down of the news, as traditional standards of journalistic objectivity give way to more subjective perspectives. This fear runs up against one of the major conceits of 20th-century journalism—that professional reporters can set aside their personal beliefs and communicate the news in an evenhanded, unbiased manner. These days, the public—and even much of the media—is increasingly skeptical of such a claim and assumes that whatever news it consumes, and what news is fed to it, is in some way tainted by the agenda of the person or organization responsible for producing it.

Another potential outgrowth of citizen journalism is that with countless volunteers covering and analyzing events, professional journalists will no longer be able to earn a living and thus the news media as it is known may cease to exist, or at least assume a much less influential form. Opening with a quote from the 16th-century English author Samuel Johnson—"No man but a blockhead ever wrote, except for money"—Thomas Kunkel, in "Express Yourself," the first selection in this chapter, contends that the citizen journalists operating today are not, in fact, blockheads destined to destroy journalism as we know it. Rather these newcomers are examples of democracy in action, performing a valuable public service, providing a check on the institutional arrogance of the news media. Far from a threat to journalism's institutions, Kunkel asserts, these pioneers are enriching news coverage and keeping the mainstream media honest.

In her expansive examination of recent developments, Ann Cooper, in "The Bigger Tent," considers the various issues arising out of the confrontation between old media and new. She concludes that, "Old media will have to let go of some attitudes and assumptions that are no longer relevant, and new media will need to recognize standards that can infuse credibility and trust into this new journalism."

Dan Gillmor describes an incident that sheds some light on what the journalism of the future may look like in the next entry, "We the Media: Grassroots Journalism By the People, For the People." During a rather dull speech by a corporate executive, Gillmor received via email a piece of information about the speaker from a blogger and posted it to his own blog. Many in the audience were on-line at the time and read the post, and the mood in the room quickly turned. The speed at which these and subsequent events transpired became what Gillmor called "a mini-legend in the business community."

Affordable video recorders and digital cameras are turning everyday people into journalists, as Allison Romano observes in "Why Everybody Is a Reporter," and traditional media outlets are encouraging them by broadcasting their coverage. "People want to feel like they are participating and we are listening," Michael Clemente, an executive producer at ABC News, states. "News should be more of a conversation than a dictation from New York."

In "The Next Big Thing in Journalism," John A. Byrne discusses an innovative project at *BusinessWeek*: a user-generated issue. The endeavor reflected what Byrne sees as an emerging movement in news gathering, one he calls the "New" New Journalism. As Byrne sees it, this new form "fully embraces its readers, treats their opinions and beliefs with respect and dignity, and leverages the intelligence of the crowd to create a more valuable outcome for all."

The blogger Kevin Drum reflects on media consolidation as well as his discipline's impact on traditional news organizations in the subsequent piece, "A Blogger Says: Save the MSM!" In the end, he predicts that in the years ahead, blogs and the mainstream media will share the same fate, and it is not likely to be a happy one. His advice: "Enjoy them while you can."

Amid all the talk about citizen journalism and the demise of big media, Alex Beam sounds a skeptical note in "Future Imperfect." He charts recent major news developments and observes that traditional journalists are still scoring the scoops. "I have seen the future, many times," he writes. "More often than not, it doesn't work." Taking a more academic and instructional approach, Greg R. Notess explores the ways in which the Web has changed how news is reported and consumed in "The Changing Information Cycle."

In the final selection in this chapter, "The Rise of the Citizen Journalist," Kenton Good discusses how citizen journalism is reshaping the news landscape and how libraries and other information hubs may be impacted.

Express Yourself*

By Thomas Kunkel
American Journalism Review, December 2006/January 2007

"No man but a blockhead ever wrote, except for money."

— Samuel Johnson

Sam, you were the original Dr. J, and your social observations were so spot-on that you occupy almost 10 pages in my "Oxford Dictionary of Quotations." Still, were you alive today, I'll bet you'd be blogging away at the DailyDoc or some such, and probably for no more money than the millions of other "blockheads" out there who are writing their noggins off.

As a card-carrying media professional, I empathize with my brethren and sistren fretting at the notion of all those semi-pros and amateurs traducing our heretofore exclusive right to decide What's Important. Who let *that* happen? I mean, wasn't somebody supposed to be guarding the door?

But, really, this must qualify as the least surprising phenomenon going. From our cave days humans have indulged a desire to let others know that we are here, that we matter. From there it's not much of a leap to "We want to be heard," and the Internet is proving to be the greatest megaphone ever devised.

Ironically, from a news standpoint, the rise of all-comers journalism is really just a circling back to our roots. We often forget that the very term stems from "journal," and what are blogs and MySpace pages but contemporary journals?

As Tom Rosenstiel and Bill Kovach reminded us in their fine book "The Elements of Journalism," this is precisely how modern news got its start. In the coffeehouses and taverns of 17th-century England, and soon after in America, visitors often recorded the news and gossip they'd picked up in their travels, personal reports that were posted for others to read. It wasn't long before some enterprising publican pulled these dispatches together into the first newspaper. And you thought OhmyNews pioneered the idea of a civilian news army! Now that same people-power fuels news sites all over the Web.

New York Times columnist Tom Friedman was here at Maryland recently, his best-seller "The World Is Flat" being our university's first-year book. He told about 1,500 young Terps that broadband and ever-faster computers have fundamentally changed our relationship with the Web, which is to say the average consumer has gone from almost exclusively downloading material to being a vigorous uploader.

Today we post our thoughts and experiences, our videos, our feedback to movies and books, our foibles and yes, even our body parts—well, thankfully, not *all* of us are posting body parts. But Friedman's point is apt: Media power is shifting from the institutional few—gulp—to the many. As he put it, "You happen to be around when Gutenberg invented the printing press."

It's a change that is frankly overdue. Media arrogance—whether reflected attitudinally (in the news pages) or institutionally (shortchanging communities in coverage)—largely gave rise to what in one sense can be interpreted as a populist backlash.

But as we are starting to figure out, the pros and the people not only can live with one another, we *need* one another. Without the reporting of mainstream journalists, what would bloggers blog about? After all, most of what we know about the public sphere is still unearthed by journalists. Then again, an emerging nation of citizen journalists is covering ignored communities, reimagining what news is, keeping a skeptical eye on the accuracy and judgment of the pros. Think not? Ask Dan Rather.

In the process they enrich the information mix. Critics Stephen Hunter of the *Washington Post* and Anthony Lane of *The New Yorker* may still be my go-to guys for movies. But Rotten Tomatoes (www.rottentomatoes.com), with its wisdom of the masses, is reliable and entertaining too, albeit in a different way.

This meeting of old and new media is an uneasy one, needless to say, in part because of the battle over agenda-setting. In late October the *Post* reported on ostensible outrage over the bluer passes of Virginia Democratic Senate candidate Jim Webb's combat novels. On the story's jump we learned that then-Senator George Allen's aides "have been trying to get other news organizations to write about the excerpts for weeks." When in frustration Webb's opponents released this "news" to Matt Drudge, it predictably prompted a talk-radio tempest, and this goofy nonstory winds up on the *Post*'s front page.

I wish the paper had had the courage to cling to its original conviction. The understandable pressure it felt belied this new media mix at its worst—not so much a world without taste as a world without judgment.

But even there, a little reflection reminds us that democracy, like a good stew, is inherently messy—and on the Web anyone can cook.

A few weeks ago another national figure, U.S. Supreme Court Justice Stephen Breyer, was on our campus. Breyer was talking about "active liberty," a phrase that, not coincidentally, is the title of his recent book. He admitted that today's blog-fueled partisanship gives him a headache, as the din can be as deafening as it is scary.

But then he thinks better of this anxiety, tells himself that the cacophony is in fact the sound of democracy. And as he said, "Better a high decibel level than none at all."

Excuse me a moment while I go upload that. . . .

The Bigger Tent[*]

By Ann Cooper
Columbia Journalism Review, September/October 2008

In the late 1990s, the staff at the Committee to Protect Journalists in New York took note of an exciting new trend in China. With traditional Chinese media under tight state censorship, people with something critical to say about their government had seized on the Internet as a new platform to publish their views. Their actions were not unlike the samizdat dissidents of the Soviet era or the poster-makers of Beijing University during the 1989 student uprising. But now, with the Internet, Chinese writers had the potential to reach a global audience.

In 1999, China arrested six people on charges of using the Internet to spread "anti-government" or "subversive" messages. I was the executive director of GPJ at the time, and we had to decide whether to take up their cases. None was a journalist in any traditional sense; reporting wasn't their daily job and they didn't write for established news organizations. But they were, we reasoned, acting journalistically. They disseminated news, information, and opinion. We took up the cases.

In the years since, CPJ has defended writers in Cuba, Iran, Malaysia, and elsewhere—some traditional journalists, some not—who used the Internet to get around official censorship. In CPJ's view, these were entrepreneurial spirits using technology to battle enemies of press freedom. The many American journalists who supported CPJ's global work readily agreed.

Yet what U.S. journalists recognized as a press-freedom breakthrough in China and Cuba looked different here at home. Here, the Internet wasn't a thrilling way to dodge government censors. It was a platform for new competitors who seemed to take particular glee in lambasting the gatekeepers of mainstream media. In the view of some online writers, American journalism was calcified, too self-important to correct its errors or own up to its biases, too pompous to talk with its audience, rather than at it. The newcomers soon surrounded the tent of traditional journalism, demanding fundamental, maybe revolutionary, change. Many inside the tent huffed that the online competitors were not "real" journalists. They were acerbic ego-trippers, publishers of opinion and unconfirmed gossip with no professional standards. They stole the hard work of mainstream reporters and rarely picked up a telephone to do their own research. Some said bloggers threatened the established order of American journalism, and maybe even American democracy.

And so it went for a few years, bloggers versus journalists; a fight over much more than semantics, a fight to see whether the big tent of American journalism would become a bigger tent to accommodate the newcomers and their new ideas. Who belongs in that tent, and who gets to decide who's in it? Put another way: Who is a journalist? It's a tantalizing question, but it's hardly worth asking anymore. *We're All Journalists Now* declared Washington lawyer Scott Gant's 2007 book, subtitled *The Transformation of the Press and Reshaping of the Law in the Internet Age*. A less sexy but perhaps more accurate title might have been, *We Can All Be Journalists, If and When We Choose to Be*. But Gant's basic point is sound; freedom of the press now belongs not just to those who own printing presses, but also to those who use cell phones, video cameras, blogging software, and other technology to deliver news and views to the world—just like those early Internet writers in China.

The expansion of the tent brings questions and challenges, of course—for institutions (who gets press passes?), for the law (how do you draft a shield bill if anyone can be a journalist?), and for journalists themselves (what are the standards of my profession?). Here's a field report—snapshots, really—on how we're all adapting to a fluid situation.

ACCESS

Soon after former radio and wire-service journalist Jim Van Dongen became a spokesman for the New Hampshire Department of Safety in 2003, he found himself confronted with press-pass applications from unpaid Internet bloggers and community-radio talk-show hosts. His first reaction: they're not "legitimate" journalists. His second reaction: we need a definition of who is.

It was Van Dongen's third reaction that was surprising. After trying out different criteria—journalists write for pay; they do original reporting, not just opinion writing—Van Dongen concluded that none of the criteria worked. In today's digital world, he says, "essentially, anybody who says he's a journalist is one." So this past January, Van Dongen's office announced that it would no longer issue press passes. "Either we must issue such ID to virtually anyone who asks for it or be placed in the position of deciding who is or is not a legitimate journalist. That is not an appropriate role for a state agency," the department said in a January 15 news advisory. Though stunning in its symbolism, the New Hampshire decision didn't have much practical effect; Safety-Department press passes were rarely needed, except for access to the state legislature floor.

Nor have other institutions rushed to copy Van Dongen's response to the credentialing dilemma. In institutional worlds such as government, politics, and business, many in charge of press operations still cast a wary eye at requests from outside mainstream media. It's not that they're inundated with applicants; many institutions say blogger requests are still something of a novelty. But they're not at all sure what to do with someone who doesn't look like a traditional journalist. Last January for example, the retail chain Target e-mailed blogger Amy Jussel to say it wouldn't answer her questions about its ad campaigns because "Target does not participate with non-traditional media outlets." Meanwhile, the New York Civil Liberties Union went to court in February to force the release of all recent New York Police Department decisions on press-pass requests; the action is aimed at determining whether, as some independent online writers claim, the NYPD denies cards to applicants who don't work in the journalistic mainstream.

But institutional barriers are definitely crumbling. Bloggers were admitted to the 2004 and 2008 political party conventions. They had reserved seating in a spillover room at the January 2007 trial of former White House aide Scooter Libby. Doors have cracked open at the United Nations, the White House, and the congressional press galleries, which have all accredited online-only journalists. So have legislatures in California, Tennessee, and Georgia, according to Michelle Blackston, a spokeswoman for the National Conference of State Legislatures. Blackston's group counsels an inclusive press policy—urging lawmakers to leak good stories to bloggers, and to start their own blogs. "We feel strongly it's a new way for lawmakers to connect with their constituents," she says.

That is precisely why barriers will continue to erode, at least for bloggers who have credibility and an audience. If their message reaches people newsmakers want to reach, their requests for press credentials and other access will be taken as seriously as those from mainstream media.

BEYOND THE SHIELD

Few issues have united mainstream media like their effort to pass a federal shield law, which would give journalists some immunity from having to reveal confidential sources to federal courts. But the number one legal issue for traditional media—which is not expected to win final congressional approval this year—hasn't stirred a lot of passion in the blogosphere, where writers attract readers with their opinionated take on events much more than with original reporting. In fact, blog writers face a very different set of legal risks from those addressed in the shield law. Bloggers, says Robert Cox, an online writer and president of the Media Bloggers Association, "are going to be intentionally provocative. They rely on hyperbole, sometimes." Cox says that several hundred lawsuits have been filed against bloggers, most charging defamation, copyright violation, or invasion of privacy.

Mainstream journalists can avoid such charges by turning to editors or in-house lawyers for advice; company insurance also provides protection if they're sued. In the blogosphere, editors are few and far between, insurance is costly, and legal help is usually limited to consulting a nonprofit resource—like Cox's group, or the Citizen Media Law Project at Harvard University. "There are some simple things bloggers can do" without compromising their passionate voices, says Cox, "but they don't know to do them." Something as basic, for example, as using the disclaimer "alleged" when writing about a person accused but not convicted of a crime. "The more professional you are, the better your standards, the more defensible your position," says Cox.

But that advice, like the online law course Cox's group plans to offer to help bloggers get insurance, isn't always well received in the fiercely independent blogosphere. "There's an extreme sensitivity to anyone trying to tell some other blogger what to do," Cox acknowledges.

I, JOURNALIST

"Bloggers vs. journalists is over," declared a January 2005 post by Jay Rosen, a journalism professor at New York University who writes prolifically about the new world of journalism at his site PressThink. "The question now isn't whether blogs can be journalism. They can be, sometimes. It isn't whether bloggers 'are' journalists. They apparently are, sometimes. We have to ask different questions now because events have moved the story forward."

When Rosen wrote that almost four years ago, events hadn't moved nearly far enough to convince many mainstream journalists that the debate was over. But in 2008, with old media in a financial crisis that seems to deepen by the week, resistance is evaporating. Traditional reporters and online writers are increasingly converging under one shared journalistic tent, where each side is free to borrow from the other. Thus, mainstream reporters still write news and analysis that strive for impartiality, but increasingly they also blog (at midsummer, nytimes.com had sixty-one news and opinion blogs; there were eighty-one at washingtonpost.com). Bloggers still aggregate and riff off the news reported in mainstream media, but a few are beginning to draw readers with original reporting.

These days it's more the act of journalism that gets you entry into the tent, not whether you're doing it every day, or doing it for pay. There are still distinctions, though. "Old" journalists are called professional, traditional, mainstream, or institutional; "new" ones are amateur, nontraditional, nonprofessional, or citizen journalists. PressThink's Rosen promotes "pro-am" experiments, in which unpaid citizen writers like Mayhill Fowler (who broke the Obama "bittergate" story for Huffington Post) work with professional editors like Marc Cooper (a journalism professor and former contributing editor at *The Nation*) to cover the news in different ways.

Does this mean we're one big happy family in the big new tent? Far from it. In an interview, Rosen said many bloggers still fume that they have second-class status; even when they break news, "there's still a sense that a story hasn't really arrived until it's picked up by the mainstream media." And while some traditionalists may be enjoying the breezier writing style that blogging allows, they wonder what it's doing to journalism's hallowed standards.

SETTING THE BAR

Last December, former NBC correspondent David Hazinski unloaded his traditional-journalist concerns on *The Atlanta Journal-Constitution*'s op-ed page. Hazinski, a journalism professor at the University of Georgia, railed against television's increasing reliance on a new form of citizen journalism—video shot by nonprofessionals, like CNN's iReports.

Calling a citizen iReporter a journalist, said Hazinski, "is like saying someone who carries a scalpel is a 'citizen surgeon' or someone who can read a law book is a 'citizen lawyer.'" What distinguishes a journalist from the average citizen who records news on his or her cell phone, said Hazinski, are education, skill, and standards. "Information without journalistic standards is called gossip," he concluded.

The blogosphere dumped a blizzard of "absolute hatred" on Hazinski. "I had death threats," he says. Most were rejecting his suggestion that a lack of standards for citizen journalism "opens up information flow to the strong probability of fraud and abuse. The news industry should find some way to monitor and regulate this new trend." The more irate responders reminded Hazinski that mainstream media's record on fraudulent reporting was far from unblemished, and that his vague call to "monitor and regulate" wasn't likely to be embraced even by mainstream journalists, in a country where the media tend to equate "regulation" of their industry with censorship.

Underneath Hazinski's provocative phrasing is an important point, though: let's not cast aside good journalism's goals and values simply because there are new ways to report and present the news. At the same time, let's do see if some of the rules need rethinking and adjustment to fit the new realities. That Mayhill Fowler article on Obama's "bitter" remarks sparked one fierce, and useful, ethical debate. Fowler recorded Obama at a fund raiser that she was able to attend only because she had contributed to his campaign, a move that violates the ethics codes of major U.S. news organizations. Yet even as Fowler's newsgathering strategies were being debated, her scoop—followed and amplified by the mainstream press— became an important new narrative in the election. No one denied that what she reported was important. "But if the old rules are fading away," wrote Michael Tomasky, who edits *Guardian America*, "there have to be a few new ones to take their place. There can't just be anarchy."

Draft ethics codes have circulated in the blogosphere, and the ideas in drafts posted at CyberJournalist.net and on the sites of bloggers such as Rebecca Blood and Tim O'Reilly would be familiar to those who've worked in major media newsrooms. It would be wrong, though, to assume that the blogosphere is likely to organize itself into mainstream-style professional groups with industry-wide standards (for that matter, mainstream media don't follow one set of standards). "The blogosphere has no organization. None. It's chaotic. That's what makes it vibrant," said Rosen.

When I asked Eric Umansky, a senior writer at the investigative journalism project ProPublica (and a CJR contributing editor) and a veteran of both old and new media, how standards of online journalism will be enforced, his answer was one that's repeated often in cyberspace: "It's going to be regulated essentially by the marketplace." That means a blog, just like a newspaper, has to build credibility; people will stop reading if it's "unreliable and unlikely to tell me anything new," he said. The marketplace solution is not particularly reassuring to many traditional journalism gatekeepers. They don't want mandatory standards, but as they open up their own thinking about the online world, they do want the blogosphere to recognize that journalism won't survive on any platform without a common belief in some principles—among them, a commitment to accuracy and to avoiding (or clearly revealing) conflicts of interest. In one of his most recent ruminations on the transitional world of journalism, Rosen described the gatekeepers as a "tribe" now migrating from the failing business model of old journalism to a new digital platform. The migration, he said, offers the opportunity to build a hybrid model with online journalists.

Rosen's hybrid notion shifts the focus from defining "who is a journalist" to "what is journalism." That's a necessary shift, and once it's made, it may be possible to build a new journalism, combining, for example, the best of traditional shoe-leather reporting with exciting new citizen-journalist teams. But a hybrid would require true collaboration between old and new practitioners who are serious about sustaining journalism and its public-service mission. Old media will have to let go of some attitudes and assumptions that are no longer relevant, and new media will need to recognize standards that can infuse credibility and trust into this new journalism. Working together will require everyone in the bigger tent to drop their animosities and check their egos. It's not about us, after all. It's about keeping watch on those in power, about ensuring an informed citizenry, about maintaining a democratic culture that is strengthened by vibrant reporting on vital institutions.

We the Media[*]

Grassroots Journalism By the People, For the People

By Dan Gillmor
Excerpted from *We the Media*, 2004

We freeze some moments in time. Every culture has its frozen moments, events so important and personal that they transcend the normal flow of news.

Americans of a certain age, for example, know precisely where they were and what they were doing when they learned that President Franklin D. Roosevelt died. Another generation has absolute clarity on their whereabouts when John F. Kennedy was assassinated. No one who was older than a baby on September 11, 2001, will ever forget hearing about, or seeing, airplanes crashed into skyscrapers.

In 1945, people gathered around radios for the immediate news, and then they stayed with the radio to hear more about their fallen leader and about the man who took his place. Newspapers printed extra editions and filled their columns with detail for days and weeks afterward. Magazines stepped back from the breaking news and offered perspective.

Something similar happened in 1963, but with a newer medium. The immediate news of Kennedy's death came for most by way of television; I'm old enough to remember that heartbreaking moment when Walter Cronkite put on his horn-rimmed glasses to glance at a message from Dallas and then, blinking back tears, told his viewers that their leader was gone. As in the earlier time, newspapers and magazines pulled out all the stops to add detail and context.

September 11, 2001, followed a similarly grim pattern. We watched—again and again—the awful events. Consumers of news learned the *what* about the attacks, thanks to the television networks that showed the horror so graphically. Then we learned some of the *how* and *why* as print publications and thoughtful broadcasters worked to bring depth to events that defied mere words. Journalists did some of their finest work and made me proud to be one of them.

But something else, something profound, was happening this time around: news was being produced by ordinary people who had something to say and show, and not solely by the "official" news organizations that had traditionally decided how the first draft of history would look. This time, the first draft of history was being written, in part, by the former audience. It was possible—it was inevitable— because of new publishing tools available on the Internet. Another kind of reporting emerged during those appalling hours and days. Via e-mails, mailing lists, chat groups, and personal Web journals—all nonstandard news sources—we received valuable context that the major American media couldn't, or wouldn't, provide. We were witnessing—and in many cases were part of—the future of news.

Six months later came another demonstration of tomorrow's journalism. The stakes were far lower this time, merely a moment of discomfort for a powerful executive. On March 26, 2002, poor Joe Nacchio got a firsthand taste of the future; this time, in a small way, I helped set the table. Actually, Nacchio was rolling in wealth that day, when he appeared at PC Forum, an exclusive executive conference in suburban Phoenix. He was also, it seemed, swimming in self-pity.

In those days, Nacchio was the chief executive of the regional telephone giant Qwest, a near-monopoly in its multistate marketplace. At the PC Forum gathering that particular day, he was complaining about difficulties in raising capital. Imagine: whining about the rigors of running a monopoly, especially when Nacchio's own management moves had contributed to some of the difficulties he was facing.

I was in the audience, reporting in something close to real time by publishing frequent conference updates on my Weblog, an online journal of short Web postings, via a wireless link the conference had set up for attendees. So was another journalist-Weblogger, Doc Searls, senior editor of *Linux Journal*, a software magazine.

Little did we know that the morning's events would turn into a mini-legend in the business community. Little did I know that the experience would expand my understanding of how thoroughly the craft of journalism was changing.

One of my posts noted Nacchio's whining, observing that he'd gotten seriously richer while his company was losing much of its market value—another example of CEOs raking in the riches while shareholders, employees, and communities got the shaft. Seconds later, I received an email from Buzz Bruggeman, a lawyer in Florida, who was following my Weblog and Searls's from his office in Orlando. "Ain't America great?" Bruggeman wrote sarcastically, attaching a hyperlink to a Yahoo! Finance Web page showing that Nacchio had cashed in more than $200 million in stock while his company's stock price was heading downhill. This information struck me as relevant to what I was writing, and I immediately dropped this juicy tidbit into my Weblog, with a cybertip of the hat to Bruggeman. ("Thanks, Buzz, for the link," I wrote parenthetically.) Doc Searls did likewise.

"Around that point, the audience turned hostile," said Esther Dyson, whose company, Edventure Holdings, held the conference.[1] Did Doc and I play a role? Apparently. Many people in the luxury hotel ballroom—perhaps half of the executives, financiers, entrepreneurs, and journalists—were also online that morning.

At least some of them were amusing themselves by following what Doc and I were writing. During the remainder of Nacchio's session, there was a perceptible chill toward the man. Dyson, an investor and author, said later she was certain that our Weblogs helped create that chill.[2] She called the blogging "a second conference occurring around, through, and across the first."

Why am I telling this story? This was not an earthshaking event, after all. For me, however, it was a tipping point. Consider the sequence of news flow: a feedback loop that started in an Arizona conference session zipped to Orlando, came back to Arizona, and ultimately went global. In a world of satellite communications and fiber optics, real-time journalism is routine; but now we journalists had added the expertise of the audience.

Those forces had lessons for everyone involved, including the "newsmaker"—Nacchio—who had to deal with new pressures on the always edgy, sometimes adversarial relationship between journalists and the people we cover. Nacchio didn't lose his job because we poked at his arrogance; he lost it, in the end, because he did an inadequate job as CEO. But he got a tiny, if unwelcome, taste of journalism's future that morning.

The person in our little story who tasted journalism's future most profoundly, I believe, was neither the professional reporter nor the newsmaker, but Bruggeman. In an earlier time, before technology collided so violently with journalism, he was a member of an audience. Now he was part of the journalistic process—in more ways than one. He received news about an event without waiting for the traditional coverage to arrive through newspapers or magazines, or even Websites. He became part of the journalistic process himself: a citizen-reporter whose knowledge and quick thinking helped inform my own journalism in a timely way.

Bruggeman was no longer just a consumer. He was a producer. He was making the news.

Journalism is transforming from a twentieth-century mass-media structure to something profoundly more grassroots and democratic. This transformation is a story, first, of evolutionary change. Humans have always told each other stories, and each new era of progress has led to an expansion of storytelling. It is, however, also a story of a modern revolution because technology has given us a communications toolkit that allows anyone to become a journalist at little cost and (in theory) with global reach. Nothing like this has ever been possible before.

In the twentieth century, making the news was almost entirely the province of journalists, the people we covered (or newsmakers), and the legions of public relations and marketing people who manipulated everyone. The economics of publishing and broadcasting created large, arrogant institutions—call them Big Media, though even small-town newspapers and broadcasters exhibit some of the phenomenon's worst symptoms. Big Media, in any event, treated the news as a lecture. We told you what the news was. You bought it, or you didn't. You might write us a letter; we might print it. (If we were television and you complained, we ignored you entirely unless the complaint arrived on a libel lawyer's letterhead.) Or you canceled your subscription or stopped watching our shows. It was a world that bred complacency and arrogance on our part. It was a gravy train while it lasted, but it was unsustainable.

Tomorrow's news reporting and production will be more of a conversation, or a seminar. The lines will blur between producers and consumers, changing the role of both in ways we're only beginning to grasp now. The communication network itself will be a medium for everyone's voice, not just the few who can afford to buy multimillion-dollar printing presses, launch satellites, or win the government's permission to squat on the public's airwaves.

This evolution—from journalism as lecture to journalism as a conversation or seminar—will force the various communities of interest to adapt. We all, from journalists to the people we cover to our sources and the former audience, must change our ways. The alternative is just more of the same.

We can't afford more of the same. We can't afford to treat the news solely as a commodity, largely controlled by big institutions. We can't afford, as a society, to limit our choices. We can't even afford it financially, because Wall Street's demands on Big Media are dumbing down the product itself.

There are three major constituencies in a world where anyone can make the news. Once largely distinct, they're now blurring into each other.

The first is journalists. We will learn we are part of something new, that our readers and listeners and viewers are becoming part of the process. I take it for granted, for example, that my readers know more than I do—and this is a liberating, not threatening, fact of journalistic life. Every reporter on every beat should embrace this. We will use the tools of grassroots journalism or be consigned to history. Our core values, including accuracy and fairness, will remain important, and we'll still be gatekeepers in some ways, but our ability to shape a larger conversation—and to provide context—will be at least as important as our ability to gather facts and report them.

The second is newsmakers. The rich and powerful are discovering new vulnerabilities, as Nacchio learned. Moreover, once anyone can be a journalist, many talented people will try—and they'll find things the professionals miss. Politicians and businesspeople are learning this every day. But newsmakers also have new ways to get out their message, using the same technologies the grassroots folks adopt. Howard Dean's presidential campaign failed, but his methods will be studied and emulated because of the way his campaign used new tools to engage his supporters in a conversation. The people at the edges of the communications and social networks can be a newsmaker's harshest, most effective critics. But they can also be the most fervent and valuable of allies, offering ideas to each other and to the newsmaker as well.

The third is the former audience. Once mere consumers of news, the audience is learning how to get a better, timelier report. It's also learning how to join the process of journalism, helping to create a massive conversation, and in some cases doing a better job than the professionals. For example, Glenn Reynolds, aka "Insta-pundit," is not just one of the most popular Webloggers; he has amassed considerable influence in the process. Some grassroots journalists will become professionals. In the end, we'll have more voices, and more options.

I've been in professional journalism for almost twenty-five years. I'm grateful for the opportunities I've had, and the position I hold. I respect and admire my colleagues, and I believe that Big Media does a superb job in many cases. But I'm absolutely certain that the journalism industry's modern structure has fostered a dangerous conservatism—from a business sense more than a political sense, though both are apparent—that threatens our future.

Our resistance to change, some of it caused by financial concerns, has wounded the journalism we practice and has made us nearly blind to tomorrow's realities. Our worst enemy may be ourselves. Corporate journalism, which dominates today, is squeezing quality to boost profits in the short run.

Perversely, such tactics are ultimately likely to undermine us.

Big Media enjoys high margins. Daily newspapers in typically quasi-monopoly markets make 25–30 percent or more in good years. Local TV stations can boast margins north of 50 percent. For Wall Street, however, no margin is sufficiently rich, and next year's profits must be higher still. This has led to a hollowing-out syndrome; newspaper publishers and broadcasting station managers have realized they can cut the amount and quality of journalism, at least for a while, to raise profits. In case after case, the demands of Wall Street and the greed of investors have subsumed the "public trust" part of journalism. I don't believe the First Amendment (which gives journalists valuable leeway to inquire and publish) was designed with corporate profits in mind. Although we haven't become a wholly cynical business yet, the trend is scary.

Consolidation makes it even more worrisome. Media companies are merging to create ever larger information and entertainment conglomerates. In too many cases, serious journalism—and the public trust—continue to be victims. All of this leaves a journalistic opening, and new journalists—especially citizen journalists—are filling the gap.

Meanwhile, even as greed and consolidation take their toll, those historically high margins are under attack. Newspapers, for example, have two main revenue streams. The smaller by far comes from circulation: readers who pay to have the paper delivered at home, or buy it from a newsstand. The larger is advertising, from employment classifieds to retail display ads, and every one of those ad revenue streams is under attack from competitors such as eBay and Craigslist, which can happily live on lower margins (or in the case of eBay, which is the world's largest classified-advertising site, establish a new monopoly) and don't care at all about journalism.

In the long run, I can easily imagine an unraveling of the business model that has rewarded me so well, and—despite the effect of excessive greed in too many executive suites—has managed to serve the public respectably in vital ways. Who will do big investigative projects, backed by deep pockets and the ability to pay expensive lawyers, when powerful interests try to punish those who exposed them, if the business model collapses? Who would have exposed the Watergate crimes in the absence of powerful publishers, especially the *Washington Post*'s Katharine Graham, who had the financial and moral fortitude to stand up to Richard Nixon and his henchmen? At a more prosaic level, who will serve, for better or worse, as a principal voice of a community or region? Flawed as we may be in the business of journalism, anarchy in news is not my idea of a solution.

A world of news anarchy would be one in which the big, credible voices of today were undermined by a combination of forces, including the financial ones I've just described. There would be no business model to support institutional journalism, which, for all its problems, does perform a public service. Credibility matters. People need, and want, trusted sources—and those sources have been, by and large, serious journalists. Instead of journalism organizations with the critical mass to fight the good fight, we may be left with the equivalent of countless pamphleteers and people shouting from soapboxes. We need something better.

Happily, the anarchy scenario doesn't strike me as probable, in part because there will always be a demand for credible news and context. Also possible, though I hope equally unlikely, is a world of information lockdown. The forces of central control are not sitting quietly, in the face of challenges to their authority.

In this scenario, we could witness an unholy alliance between the entertainment industry—what I call the "copyright cartel"—and government. Governments are quite uneasy about the free flow of information, and they allow it only to a point. Legal clampdowns and technological measures to prevent copyright infringement could bring a day when we need permission to publish, or when publishing from the edge feels too risky. The cartel has targeted some of the essential innovations of tomorrow's news, such as the peer-to-peer file sharing that does make infringement easier but also gives citizen journalists one of the only affordable ways to distribute what they create. Governments insist on the right to track everything we do, but more and more politicians and bureaucrats shut off access to what the public needs to know—information that increasingly surfaces through the efforts of nontraditional media.

In short, we cannot just assume that self-publishing from the edges of our networks—the grassroots journalism we need so desperately—will survive, much less thrive. We will need to defend it, with the same vigor we defend other liberties. Instead of a news anarchy or lockdown, I seek a balance that simultaneously preserves the best of today's system and encourages tomorrow's emergent, self-assembling journalism.

It won't be immediately workable for the people who already get so little attention from Big Media. Today, citizen journalism is mostly the province of what my friend and former newspaper editor Tom Stites calls "a rather narrow and very privileged slice of the polity—those who are educated enough to take part in the wired conversation, who have the technical skills, and who are affluent enough to have the time and equipment." These are the very same people we're leaving behind in our Brave New Economy. They are everyday people, buffeted by change, and outside the conversation. To our discredit, we have not listened to them as well as we should have.

The rise of the citizen-journalist will help us listen. The ability of anyone to make the news will give new voice to people who've felt voiceless—and whose words we need to hear. They are showing all of us—citizen, journalist, newsmaker—new ways of talking, of learning.

In the end, they may help spark a renaissance of the notion, now threatened, of a truly informed citizenry. Self-government demands no less, and we'll all benefit if we do it right.

Let's have this conversation, for everyone's sake.

NOTES

1. Esther Dyson's column about the Nacchio incident can be found at http://www.edventure.com/conversation/article.cfm?Counter=8648145.

2. I'm convinced Nacchio was perfectly capable of annoying the audience all by himself. Clay Shirky, also in the room that day, felt the mood shifting and wondered why, until someone pointed out the blogging on a nearby computer screen. He told me: "Now, normally, a blog entry like this would take a day or so to ripple outwards, but because this was such a wired crowd and, frankly, because Nacchio's talk was so dull, a lot of people were catching up on their blog reading during the talk, and even people not reading were near people who were. So the whole thing, from discovery to publication to spread, got really compressed, and basically happened during the time he was onstage. The capper was when Dennis Kneale [from *Forbes* magazine] got up at question time, offered mock sympathy for Nacchio's plight, and then ended by asking 'What can we do for you?' By that point, the mood of the room had gone from 'Good Lord, this is boring' to 'Why isn't that guy in jail?'"

Why Everybody Is a Reporter[*]

By Allison Romano
Broadcasting & Cable, August 22, 2005

Paul Chenoweth never leaves home without his digital camera or video camera. A graduate student at Belmont University in Nashville, Tenn., he shoots video and photos around town and posts them to his technology-themed Weblog, Chasing the Dragon's Tail. Chenoweth is particularly proud of a piece he filmed recently in Rio das Pedras, Brazil, where a group from the local Brentwood Baptist Church helped construct a new church.

Chenoweth is not a reporter or cameraman but a one-man news crew among a growing number of citizen journalists now exploiting the efficiency of cheap, portable gadgets and the instant speed and spread of publishing on the Internet, particularly on Web logs (or blogs). It's vox populi meets reality TV.

For some, it means picking up a camera and supplying pictures and video to a local TV station. Others are going a step further, creating their own mini news organizations with pictures, news stories and video clips of events in their communities—anything from softball games to town-council meetings.

Budget-conscious stations, lured by the prospect of beating the competition, are willing enablers. In a twist, a handful of mainstream news outlets not only are using amateur footage but are also training contributors in basic journalism.

In cities from Bakersfield, Calif., to Greensboro, N.C., residents have started hyper-local Web sites that go into minute detail about at-home happenings. One such Web site, Denver-based Yourhub.com, also publishes weekly supplements for the *Rocky Mountain News*. A handful of radio stations are even coaching listeners on how to be hosts and reporters.

Traditional journalists and media companies say these newcomers aren't true journalists. And, though they occasionally break news, citizen journalists lack the resources to be reliable and often get facts wrong.

But the trend doesn't show any signs of abating. In October, University of Maryland's Institute for Interactive Journalism will host the first-ever "citizen's media" convention, which will, in part, advise individuals on how to start up and execute newsgathering and reporting in their own communities.

"Many neighborhoods and towns are not terribly well-covered by the mainstream media," says Rich Gordon, head of the new-media program at Northwestern University's Medill School of Journalism, in part because it is difficult for news organizations to financially support staffing in suburban and rural areas. But taking contributions from locals, Gordon says, could be a solution that would give communities more exposure and provide TV outlets with free or low-cost coverage.

That sentiment is expressed in Nashville, too. "There are other people besides journalists that have a voice," Chenoweth says, "and they aren't being heard on the news."

So far, the most high-profile effort to recruit audience participation is not in news but from a cable entertainment channel. At newly launched Current, which is geared toward young adults and backed by former Vice President Al Gore and legal-services mogul Joel Hyatt, about 25% of its programming is "viewer-created content"—short-form pieces created by Current's 18–34 core audience. To get on the air, viewers submit their work online for peer review, and Current staffers scour the feedback and select work to air.

Yasmin Vossoughian, a 26-year-old aspiring journalist and filmmaker, submitted a short documentary to Current on women in Iran that she filmed while visiting family members there. She says viewers can help bring more perspective to TV: "So many times I'm watching the news, and I'm like, 'God, I would've done it like this,' or, 'Why aren't they showing subjects like this?'"

Current's "v-c squared" model, the channel's buzzword for its viewer-submitted content, consists of mini-documentaries that are more likely to come from aspiring filmmakers. But TV networks and stations across the country are clamoring for more audience participation.

The proliferation of new technology is making such efforts possible. More than 60 million Americans own video camcorders. Cellphones with built-in cameras are flooding the market. This year, almost half of the cellphones sold in North America will come with cameras. Cellphone maker Nokia now says it is the largest manufacturer of digital cameras in the world, elbowing out traditional camera companies. And, says WABC New York News Director Kenny Plotnick, "Anyone with a camera is tantamount to being a reporter."

Citizen journalism seemed to reach critical mass this summer when suicide bombers attacked London's transportation system. On shattered subway cars, victims recorded the aftermath on their cellphones and e-mailed dark, grainy video and still pictures to British TV networks. It was the first time cellphone video had been widely used to cover a major news story. A month later, when an Air France jumbo jet careened off the runway in Toronto, shaken passengers once again took out their cellphones and started recording. The recent earthquake in Tokyo yielded the same results.

These events inspired many newsrooms to advertise for content. The national news networks began asking viewers to send in breaking-news images and video. A handful of TV stations, from big-market players like WABC to smaller outlets such as WTKR Norfolk, Va., also put out the call. Most say they'd be willing to pay for video—up to several hundred dollars—to secure exclusivity. Still, liability over such issues as privacy rights and defamation has yet to be settled.

TV reporters are testing out their own portable gadgets. ABC, CBS and NBC are handing out video-enabled cellphones to staffers. Later this year, ABC's 24/7 broadband and cable network, ABC News Now, plans to outfit some reporters with Nokia's new $900 N90, which the manufacturer says shoots VHS-quality video.

But news executives are divided on how much of a role the audience should play. Chief among their concerns: the quality and authenticity of video and pictures that viewers send in. "These are not journalists, and that scares me," says Steve Schwaid, head of programming and news for NBC's owned-and-operated stations. "How do I know what training they've had and what their relationships are?"

Another dilemma, news managers say, is that overly eager people could become community paparazzi, getting too close to victims or disrupting police work. "In television, we have sensibilities about shooting video," says TV-news consultant Valerie Hyman. "We mute the sound or shoot from far away. People in the general public have none of that discussion—and who would expect them to? They're not journalists."

FIGHT FOR ATTENTION

And yet the desire to be first is palpable. If one news outlet won't take the video, there are dozens more that might. Networks and stations are fighting with cable channels and the Internet for viewers' attention.

Audience participation and so-called "grassroots journalism" also present a novel way to connect with the audience. "When you have millions of people armed with cameras that may find great stories, it is important you are the place they want to turn it over to," says Mark Antonitis, president/general manager for Young Broadcasting's KRON San Francisco.

Once the video or pictures are shot, specialized Internet sites and low-cost production tools enable regular citizens to easily publish their own blogs and news sites. Flickr.com, a photo-sharing service recently acquired by Yahoo, allows users to share photos and commentary; Blinkx.tv lets users search thousands of podcasts and video blogs. Yahoo recently launched My Web 2.0, message boards for people with common interests, and Google is adding video searches. Scoopt, a Glasgow, Scotland-based startup, helps people sell their cellphone pictures or video, although it keeps half the proceeds.

TV-news professionals are still trying to "grok" the blogosphere. Political blog-gers reported on the presidential campaign with unrivaled zeal, covering the Dem-ocratic and Republican National Conventions for the first time. CNN added a segment on political blogs to its afternoon show Inside Politics, and ABC News Now handed out Sprint cellphone cameras to people marching in the inaugural parade, then aired their video and pictures.

A handful of TV-news companies are cultivating relationships with contribu-tors. Regional cable news channel New England Cable News (NECN) asks view-ers to contribute local stories, such as promising-athlete profiles or traffic-snarl reports. "Viewers are always saying the stories that we do don't reflect their lives," says Steve Safran, director of digital media. "OK, so what's going on in your life? Tell us. We can't be everywhere at once, but you can." NECN carefully distinguish-es the amateur video from that of its own journalists, opting to call the sources "citizen newsgatherers."

In Nashville, WKRN is going a step further. The station not only is soliciting video but is also training locals. In July, it hosted 20 area bloggers, including Che-noweth, for a crash course in video production. At the workshop, station photog-raphers gave instruction on basic videography and critiqued the students' work. "The biggest problem is that people shoot great images but it's shaky and they zoom in and out," says Terry Heaton, a TV-news consultant working with WKRN. "If they find themselves in a spot-news situation, we want it to be usable."

The workshop also gives WKRN a chance to screen bloggers as potential sourc-es. "We've started relationships with them," says station President Mike Sechrist. For example, he says, "if Paul [Chenoweth] sent me video, I'd have high confi-dence using it."

TRAINING CITIZEN JOURNALISTS

The BBC is incorporating local contributors into its newsrooms. Under a new pilot program, the broadcaster is launching 60 stations and plans to have com-munity reporters generate one-fifth of the content. Michael Rosenblum, a former CBS news executive and news consultant, is working with the BBC on the effort and recommends that American news outlets pursue a similar tactic: "Technical training and baseline journalism training are critical."

Before e-mail and cellphone messaging, if an individual had hot video, news managers recall, they would often bring it into the newsroom themselves. Now content is relayed anonymously. Generally, news executives will ask e-mailers to send their phone number so they can be quickly interviewed. Contributors are usually required to sign documents attesting that the content is genuine. On-air, an anchor might identify the content as viewer-contributed, and on-screen graphics can reinforce the separation. Says Eric Braun, former head of news for Raycom Media's broadcast-station group and now managing editor of AP's international

TV operation, "We have to apply all the same checks and balances as we do with our own editorial content—and more."

"MORE OF A CONVERSATION"

Even with safeguards in place, news executives worry that questionable content could slip through. "There are a lot of unscrupulous people out there that could be trying to dupe a news organization," says Marcy McGinnis, senior VP of newsgathering for CBS News.

Despite any misgivings, McGinnis and others say they want more viewer involvement. "People want to feel like they are participating and we are listening," says ABC News Now executive producer Michael Clemente. "News should be more of a conversation than a dictation from New York."

The Next Big Thing in Journalism[*]

By John A. Byrne
Christian Science Monitor, September 8, 2008

Print media are reeling. The pace of financial losses and massive layoffs is accelerating. Panic is setting in.

It's easy to blame the Web for this bleak picture. But the same disruptive technology that has caused such dismay in print is also ushering in the most creative period in the history of journalism.

If this were the Renaissance, the Web would be Florence, a place of amazing experimentation where all the old mediums—in this case, print, radio, and television—suddenly converge in one dynamic and democratic place. Yet, the multimedia dimensions of digital journalism are only part of the story. The most powerful attribute of this new journalism is how it directly engages our readers as active participants at every stage of content creation.

For the past year, this has become the passion and focus of BusinessWeek, where I serve as executive editor: It's to reinvent journalism as a process that involves the reader in the front end, to advocate story ideas; in the middle, to inform the reporting of a story; and in the end, to expand on the conversation a story creates. That latter conversation is not a letter-to-the-editor monologue, but rather a dialogue between the professional writers and the audience.

In the early 1960s, Tom Wolfe and other talented writers created the New Journalism. It cleverly deployed the techniques of great fiction to news and feature writing. Today's direct engagement with readers is the antithesis of Mr. Wolfe's self-centered narrative inventions. Call it the "New" New Journalism.

It fully embraces its readers, treats their opinions and beliefs with respect and dignity, and leverages the intelligence of the crowd to create a more valuable outcome for all. It recognizes that content is no longer king; Context is. In a world of commoditization, where too much news and opinion already chases too few eyeballs, this new loyalty-inducing journalism builds community and relationships.

But it's no cakewalk. For the past nine months, we've been aggressively promoting the smartest observations by readers on our stories, encouraging them to send us their story ideas, asking—through blogs—for their participation in stories in progress, inviting them to write guest columns, and urging our journalists to engage in direct conversations with users. In short, we're turning our readers into citizen editors.

All of these efforts culminated in a user-generated issue of BusinessWeek, "Trouble at the Office," which recently hit newsstands, as well as a major new online feature called the "Business Exchange" that debuts Monday. Business Exchange will allow users to create their own topics of interest; write headlines and blurbs to self-selected news and analysis from all over the Web; and, through their actions, decide which stories get placed on a "front page."

What have we learned? The "New" New Journalism takes work, a lot more work than traditional writing and editing.

"Trouble at the Office," for example, involved interactions with well over 10,000 readers. So it required twice the editorial workload of a conventional effort. Soliciting participation was hard; vetting and structuring it was even harder. And the usual give-and-take between a writer and an editor gets lengthened when working with amateurs.

Even though we spent four months on this user-generated issue, it was tough to get the flow going. Readers are busy people doing other things—that is, things other than reporting, thinking deeply about a narrow subject, and writing cogently about it. We should have started earlier and seeded discussions with our own provocative essays, podcasts, and videos to give people an idea of what we were looking for.

And there are limitations. In general, a reader's ability to offer a smart, impassioned response to a problem, especially about something as personal as their job and career, rarely translates into an ability to write a long-form piece. Remember: they're not pros. We had too many editors wanting to rewrite the voice out of the contributions. It's more important to preserve the readers' voice and the passion.

Participatory journalism also works best for subjects on which readers have authority. That is why the workplace was a fertile area of experimentation. Asking our readers to write on how to fix the subprime mess might not add much.

That said, I've been utterly transformed by embracing an intelligent and thoughtful audience. We've learned that they are passionate, willing to share valuable thoughts and insights, generous with their effort and time. What's more, engaging users in the reinvention of our craft has led to the discovery that our readers are exactly like us: They share a common goal to improve life, not merely bringing issues and situations to light, but sharing and working toward common solutions. That is the true essence of community.

A Blogger Says: Save the MSM!*

By Kevin Drum
Mother Jones, March/April 2007

There's an intriguing paradox at the heart of the modern trend toward media consolidation, one that my great-grandfather probably would have appreciated. You see, around the turn of the last century Eli Drum was the editor and sole proprietor of the weekly *Cerro Gordo Star*, and even in tiny Cerro Gordo, Illinois (pop. 1,000 in its heyday), Eli had competition: his archrival, the *New Era*. In all, rural Piatt County supported nearly a dozen papers, and in the entire country there were probably 15,000 or more. That's a lot of newspapers.

Since then, of course, the newspaper industry has consolidated dramatically, a trend that's accelerated in the past decade. But in practical terms, just the opposite has happened. After all, who cares if there were 15,000 tiny newspapers 100 years ago? If you were an actual person who lived in the actual town of Cerro Gordo in the actual year 1900, your only real choice was between two newspapers, each with four pages of boilerplate provided by a big-city daily and four pages printed by a local press, delivered to your doorstep once a week. And that was it.

Thirty years ago things were better, but in practice most people still had pretty limited access to news even then: one or two newspapers, three TV networks, and a few national newsmagazines.

And today? The number of independent media companies may be a fraction of what it was 30 or 100 years ago, but for no more than the price of an AOL account we have instant entrée to every single one of them. So while there may be half as many American correspondents in Moscow as there were three decades ago, back then I had access to no more than two or three of them. Today I have access to all of them. In practical terms, there's a far larger assortment of news sources available to me than 30 years ago.

As a full-time blogger, I confront this every day. In the course of a single month, on just one blog, I gather—and comment on—news from 10 to 20 American newspapers; four or five overseas papers; transcripts of radio shows, TV news, and chat shows; and at least a dozen magazines. I am awash in news.

In a very real sense, this makes blogs a powerful antidote to media consolidation. If you read a few well-chosen blogs daily, you'll find links and commentary to a far wider variety of news sources than even the best-read news consumer of a mere decade ago. You may not personally read the *Wall Street Journal, Vanity Fair,* the *Los Angeles Times,* and the *Guardian,* but the blogosphere does, and if any one of these publications has something original to say on the news of the day, blogs will compile their insights for you, complete with links to the original sources.

However, this is where our initial paradox circles back on its own tail. One of the most valuable things I do as a blogger is read five or six news accounts of the same event and then present to my readers the bits and pieces that illuminate one another (something the old media almost never does because professional reporters—still hostage to a scoop-based mentality their readers no longer care about—are loath to even admit the existence of their competitors). This form of blogging helps mask the reality of media consolidation by searching out different takes on the news, but if consolidation continues apace, eventually even blog aggregation won't be able to hide what's happening.

It also highlights why blogs—or "citizen journalism" to its most enthusiastic cheerleaders—will never replace the mainstream media (a term so prevalent it has its own IM-like abbreviation: MSM). For all the hype over blogosphere triumphs such as the takedown of Dan Rather or the almost instant posting of cell-phone photos of the 2004 tsunami, the plain fact is that very few blogs do sustained original reporting of their own. It's also why the endless debate over whether blogs are better or worse than the MSM is pointless. In the same way that newspapers excel at broad coverage of breaking news, TV excels at images, magazines excel at long analytic pieces, and talk radio excels at ranting screeds, blogs also excel at certain things. Trying to compare them to "journalism" is a mug's game, like trying to figure out if a beanbag is really a chair. Who cares? Beanbags are great for certain forms of sitting down and lousy at others.

In fact, blogs and the MSM are symbiotic. Blogs at their best improve on MSM reporting both by holding reporters to account and by latching onto complex topics and talking about them in a conversational style that professional reporters just can't match. But the blogosphere would shrivel and die without a steady diet of news reporting from paid professionals.

Which leads us to the dirty little secret of newsgathering: Serious, daily, national reporting is overwhelmingly the preserve of a tiny handful of big-city newspapers with large staffs and worldwide bureaus. Of these, the *Los Angeles Times* is under pressure to downsize by its parent company, as is the *Washington Post.* Knight Ridder was recently purchased by McClatchy. And every big-metro daily in the country, including the still-independent *New York Times,* is under relentless pressure from deteriorating circulation, poor demographics, loss of classified ad revenue to the Internet, and the decline of urban department stores—storms that private owners might have weathered but institutional investors have no stomach for.

When these dailies succumb, there's really nothing to replace them. Television news does very little in-depth daily reporting, most radio is hopeless, and blogs simply don't have the resources. Magazines do some good work but come out only weekly or monthly. So while the raw numbers of media consolidation may be the most dramatic symptom of the problem, it's the small number of national dailies at the core of today's MSM that ought to be the biggest cause for concern. And when they go? For the most part, blogs will go with them. Enjoy them while you can.

Future Imperfect[*]

By Alex Beam
The Boston Globe, August 25, 2009

I forgive you in advance if you missed Chadwick Matlin's recent article in The Big Money, an online business magazine. Matlin announced that a new Web application called HuffPost Social News, a partnership between Facebook and the Huffington Post website, is "the future of journalism."

Forget about how Social News works. It assumes, for starters, that you rely on the Huffington Post for news. It's the larger concept: "the future of journalism." Haven't I heard that somewhere before?

Well, yes.

Remember VuText? Of course you don't. Before the dawn of time, during the 1980s, Knight-Ridder (once an important newspaper chain; sheesh! do I have to explain everything?) had this idea of sending digitized news articles to people's personal computers. There were just a couple of problems. First, not that many people owned PCs, and those who did were mainly running VisiCalc, WordPerfect, and Lotus 1-2-3 on them. For the average consumer, the Internet didn't exist.

Reality 1, Future of Journalism 0.

Around the same time, the Christian Science Church lost its shirt pumping tens of millions of dollars down the dry well of . . . the future of journalism. The Scientists had it all figured out: Multimedia platforms rule! They had an international radio network, a famous newspaper, and a TV station with correspondents all over the world.

All they needed was an audience. It never came.

What about Microsoft Sidewalk? I remember when that was the future of journalism, and every newspaper in America was going weak at the knees. Microsoft was gobbling up journalistic talent, to launch category-killing city websites that would blow print media out of the water. According to a 1996 memo obtained by The Wall Street Journal, "Microsoft will soon add real estate listings, classified advertising, and consumer guides that combine Yellow Page-style listings with product reviews and promotions" to Sidewalk.

Where is Sidewalk today? To paraphrase Joseph Conrad: Mr. Sidewalk, he dead. Where is the daily newspaper? To paraphrase the boozy, woozy, embattled hoofer in Stephen Sondheim's lovely musical "Follies": We're still here.

Do you recall "civic journalism"? What a howler that was. Flush with foundation money, newspapers and other media convened snoozola focus groups to lecture voters on issues the media deemed to be important. Then we covered the focus groups! That was a lot easier than, say, traveling all the way to New Hampshire to find out what voters were interested in.

I'm not sure the genre ever recovered from Michael Kelly's withering doorslammer in The New Yorker, where he took on "the do-gooding philosophy known variably as 'civic journalism' and 'public journalism.'" "At the core of the idea there was always a fraud," Kelly wrote in an article partially attributing the re-election of the racist North Carolina Senator Jesse Helms to new media eyewash. "The fraud was the notion that a self-selected group of reporters and editors somehow could or should determine the fit subjects for debate in an election."

I suppose civic journalism has morphed into laughable "citizens" journalism, where random jokers point their cellphones at news events and dilate accordingly. Did you follow the Huffington Post's inane "citizen ground level campaign coverage" feature "Off the Bus" last year? Don't feel bad; no one else did either.

Reality 5, Future of Journalism 0.

So what will the future of journalism look like? As do all futures, it will encompass the past. Who has helped send three successive speakers of the Massachusetts House to the penalty box? We have. Who learned about the National Security Agency's warrantless wiretapping of American citizens? A reporter for The New York Times. Who chased down blubbering cricketeer-Ponzi swindler Allen Stanford? A reporter for ABC News, another beleaguered member of the mainstream media.

Who broke the news about John Edwards's adultery and the ensuing mountain of backstopping lies? Not the triumphalist, self-aggrandizing political bloggers: "a total [bleep] story"—MyDD.com; "The wingnutisphere is in a tizzy"—Daily Kos. It was a couple of newshounds from the National Enquirer, the same people who reported the heck out of the O. J. Simpson story back in the day. In business for over 80 years, and still a force to be reckoned with.

To recap: I have seen the future, many times. More often than not, it doesn't work.

The Changing Information Cycle[*]

By Greg R. Notess

Online (Weston, Conn.), September/October 2004

I have been pondering the whole concept of the role of the changing information cycle. After years of playing around on the Net, searching for information, evaluating Web sites, comparing tools, and investigating the changing online information universe, I've realized that the information journey on the Internet differs from a similar search in bibliographic or full-text databases. There, a typical research process revolves around articles and books, and knowledge of the traditional information cycle helps determine which source may have the most relevant information.

On the Internet, the traditional information cycle is broken in a variety of ways. News may be reported, analyzed, debated, corrected, and reinterpreted in a matter of hours. Old stories from decades ago may be re-examined. Factual information can be evaluated, expanded upon, and expounded on by a wide variety of readers.

Instead of reading through complete Web pages or sites, searchers can browse results and choose to read a variety of extracts from pages created by completely different organizations. Finding a community of Web sites that together provide an answer can offer a deeper and broader understanding of certain issues.

THE WEB AS INFORMATION COMMUNITY

The Web has succeeded so spectacularly as a new publishing and communication medium for many reasons—the ease with which anyone can publish, the ability to change and update content, the interconnectedness from linking, the lack of a limit to the quantity of information published, and more. While many Web sites, including some of the most popular ones, continue to use the print model of publishing information in somewhat static articles, others are experimenting

---

[*] First published by Information Today, Inc., www.infotoday.com. All rights reserved. Used with permission.

with improving overall information quality by having broader participation in the writing, correcting, and updating of content.

With the linking patterns on the Web, sites can create virtual communities of interlinked sites that provide different views, related information, and varying interpretations while still linking to each other. Following the links between the sites can create a more complete information portrait of an issue.

SINGLE SOURCE DOMINANCE

Still, for many online information seekers, a single source information focus remains. When an information need is of relatively low value, a single Web page will satisfy most users. Simply looking for the stars in the movie *Rear Window*, the meaning of "photosphere," or the five stages of grief? A Web search on any of these will pull up plenty of pages, all of which will probably have a correct answer. For those just looking for answers for their own curiosity, to help a friend, or on a whim, the single page can work.

For information professionals, there are times when an answer on a single page may suffice, but more often confirmation from several diverse sources helps confirm authenticity of the information. Yet with the Web, authenticity and accuracy is always questionable. Many pages, even from reliable organizations, have typographical errors and misstatements of fact. It is so easy to post a Web page that much Web content fails to have significant editorial oversight.

VARIABLE CONTENT

For example, in looking for an explanation of a biological process, a USGS (U.S. Geological Survey) Web page (from the biology side, not the geology side) gave one explanation that did not match the text of the search query. Checking the current page against older copies from the Wayback Machine showed that there had been a small change on the page—a "not" had been removed. This small removal completely changed the explanation of the process, and made it match the definition from other reputable sources. But it goes to show how even reputable, often authoritative organizations can make simple errors on Web pages.

Consider someone looking for the Spanish way of saying "happy birthday." Many Web pages contain the Spanish phrase, but different ones have variations such as

¡Feliz cumpleaõs!
Feliz Cumplean~os!
Feliz cumpleanos

The diacritic mark may be left out on some sites or may not display correctly.

In both these cases, trusting a single page, no matter how reliable the organization, can lead to incorrect information. Fortunately, the Web makes it easy to move beyond the single article focus.

BENEFITS OF MULTIPLE RESULTS

Search engines typically default to showing 10 results to a query, with Yahoo!'s default of 20 a welcome exception. Yet even with just 10 results, the results should be scanned to see how much difference they provide in their answers. Using an advanced search form, or the preferences to display more results, helps to further explore the possibility of conflicting or contradictory information.

Both of these examples showed a variety of conflicting answers in the results list. This led to the exploration of the contradictory or conflicting answers which when combined with evaluating the sources, comparing wording, and checking the frequency of the various answers, helped deduce the most likely correct answer to each.

THE BATHTUB QUESTION

The ability to triangulate on the Web and use multiple sources to come up with an answer is often much easier than it is to do in books and articles. Take for example the highly entertaining, if somewhat trivial, issue of when the first bathtub appeared in the White House. In the print era of book and article dominance, H. L. Mencken wrote an article for New York's *Evening Mail* in 1917. It discussed the "history" of the first bathtubs in America and the controversy around the installation of the first one at the White House by Millard Fillmore. The only problem is that this article by Mencken was fiction. After finding his "history" had been quoted as fact by other writers, Mencken wrote another article in 1926 in the *Chicago Tribune* as a public confession that his earlier piece was pure fiction and explained his reasons. Note that this took 8 years in the print age of the article.

By that point, his earlier fiction had been repeated so often that it continues to this day to appear in reputable reference sources, in print and online. Grolier's encyclopedias, the *Washington Post*, and the Internet Public Library [www.ipl.org/div/potus/mfillmore.html] have all taken information from that oft-repeated 1917 article and treated it as fact. For more information on this, see the book *The Bathtub Hoax, and Other Blasts & Bravos from the Chicago Tribune* by Mencken and the Web page, "Millard Fillmore's Bathtub" [www.sniggle.net/bathtub.php], which lists many places that have repeated the falsehoods.

Note the difference with how the Web can handle this kind of situation. Searching for white house bathtub at Yahoo!, Google, or Teoma finds a collection of Web pages including the Sniggle.net page and ones that credit Fillmore or even his successor Pierce for some reason. One of the best results for this question comes from a page that reprints a 1990 article from *Plumbing and Mechanical* on the history of plumbing in the White House. It discusses the hoax along with earlier reports of tubs in the White House. But for this question, no one single Web page really answers this question well. It is the sum total of the Web pages, incorrect and accurate, along with the reproduced articles that really help answer this question.

COMMENTS AND CORRECTIONS

It is the ability of the new online environment to quickly and easily correct, or at least criticize, information that makes the online medium so different from print. One problem with the published world of information as seen in books and periodicals is that despite editing, fact checking, and the peer review process, all kinds of errors still found their way into print, as the Mencken hoax illustrates. Periodicals would use errata sections to correct some of the errors, and letters to the editor could be used to debate a previous article's contentions and possibly set the record straight.

Unfortunately, many readers would never see errata and letters that, by the necessity of the printing process, would appear in subsequent issues of the periodical. While some indexes did a great job of combining both original article and errata and follow-up letters in the same section of the index, this only helps if the reader used the index to get to the material (and understood how to interpret those index entries). If the reader arrived at the original article by browsing or from a citation in another source, there would be no obvious connection to the corrections.

As for books, authors could and can write whatever they please, subject only to whatever editorial oversight the publisher exerts. The reader can look for book reviews that might criticize the information quality and compare it to other similar books, but, again, the reader needs to know how to find book reviews.

On the Web, the online publication format allows for much easier use of comments and corrections, and, indeed, this aspect is one of the great advances that Web publishing has to offer. The ease of publishing on the Net is such that if someone posts something obviously erroneous, someone else can easily post a rebuttal, refutation, or correction. Online periodicals can be sure to link corrections and letters to the original article. They can even remove or change previously published articles.

Elsewhere on the Internet, comments and links to related information are common. Discussions in Usenet news, Web forums, and mailing lists help give context, and reviews on commercial sites like Amazon and Epinions provide new information content. Weblogs offer easy content posting with the ability for others to add comments. Blogs also allow the original author to change their content. This cycle of comments, corrections, and changes is part of the changing information cycle on the Net.

WEBLOGS AND WIKIS

Prominent on many Weblogs is the opportunity for readers to add their own comments. Added to the nature of many blogs to link to other related postings, this creates a virtual community that (sometimes) provides a larger picture of an issue than any one single posting.

Consider also the Wikipedia, a collaborative encyclopedia writing project that uses wiki software to let anyone add and correct information. Active since 2001, it now has over 290,000 articles, many of which not only rank well in search engine results but also contain some quality writing and a good source for many kinds of information. It also incorporates comments under a "discussion" tab. For example, the article on Brazil has comments about the copyright status of the map used in the article and the validity of a description of one of the languages [http://en.wikipedia.org/wiki/Talk:Brazil].

Slashdot, a site for news and discussion among the technologically inclined, is a very active site with comments being a major component. The posting about the launch of the Public Library of Science [http://slashdot.org/science/03/10/13/119223.shtml] has over 100 comments from the mundane to the insightful.

EXPANSION OF CONTENT

The ability to comment and correct information can be useful in a variety of settings. Consider the typical computer software documentation. Whether in print or online, few are well written, and almost none are comprehensive. The better documentation is well-organized and goes into some depth on the program capabilities and features.

The difficulty is often that such documentation cannot include all possible errors or anticipate all questions. So why not make it a bit more interactive? The MySQL online manual with annotations does just that [http://dev.mysql.com/doc/mysql/en/]. The manual has a user comment box available at the end of each section. Previous user comments about the section are displayed along with an option to add new ones. Some comments try to clarify language. Others give examples, while a few mention situations where the program will work a bit differently than described in the documentation.

RETRAINING FOR COMMUNITY READING

Not all Internet content is published in this communal environment, nor is it necessary for many types of information. Yet for those of us used to the more bounded research process using indexes, periodical articles, and books, it is worth considering the differences with the information cycle on the Net.

When under the pressure of the clock, or the urgent user, it is easy to skim over comments, to only look at the first few results, to take the first answer presented online. Instead, I find that I am working on retraining myself to dig more deeply on the Web, to look more broadly at the range of answers, and to search for the combination of resources that gives a more knowledgeable answer. Much of that retraining involves looking at comments critically, to track links in both directions, to seek out divergent views, and to evaluate much of the content based on the Internet's information cycle rather than the print information cycle.

The Rise of the Citizen Journalist*

By Kenton Good
Feliciter, 2006

So there I was, at the corner of Queen and Yonge, desperately looking for a creative way to capture your attention. And then it hit me! The headline from the January 31st *Toronto Star*: "A nasty brawl between a motorist and a bike courier in Kensington Market has become a major hit on the Internet after photos of the incident were posted on blogs."[1]

The Kensington Market brawl story is one small example of citizen journalism—labelled participatory journalism by Shayne Bowman and Chris Willis, authors of "We Media: How Audiences Are Shaping the Future of News and Information." Bowman and Willis define participatory journalism as: "The act of a citizen, or group of citizens, playing an active role in the process of collecting, reporting, analyzing and disseminating news and information. The intent of this participation is to provide independent, reliable, accurate, wide-ranging and relevant information that a democracy requires."[2]

Citizen journalism, enabled by an explosion of free publishing tools, is influencing traditional media and giving an independent voice for points of view previously disenfranchised by the corporate media. Librarians have an opportunity and responsibility to incorporate citizen journalism into our library services and collections.

AN ANTIDOTE TO CONVERGENCE

Citizen journalism empowers the average person to become a journalist and share their voice. At its most basic, it requires nothing more than access to the Internet and the ability to publish to it. Signing up for a free blog account is only one of many options to start the process. The citizen journalist has the power to break a story, create some attention for that story in the blogosphere and, if the

* This article was originally published in *Feliciter*, the magazine of the Canadian Library Association, Vol. 52 No. 2 (April 2006)

story develops some traction, influence the corporate media into covering that story. Citizen journalism delivers on the original promise of the web as a democratic enabler. It is looked upon by some as an antidote to the narrowing of voice currently found in the converging corporate media.

Critics of citizen journalism, like critics of the wildly popular Wikipedia project, point to the issue of authority. How are we to tell whether the story is factually correct? And what about objectivity? Is the author approaching the story with the same objectivity that traditional media outlets theoretically attempt to achieve? Indeed, the quality of citizen journalism can vary widely, from former print journalists freelancing in the world of citizen journalism to extremist groups with clear and not so hidden agendas.

The citizen journalism tool kit is accessible and inexpensive. Free or low-cost publishing tools (e.g. blogs, RSS and tagging), blog content aggregation services such as Technorati, and photo-sharing services such as Flickr[3] are just a few examples of the tools required to be a citizen journalist. Inexpensive digital cameras and the ubiquitous wireless and mobile devices for quick publishing to the web further round out this toolkit. Given that the core components of this toolkit are free and that libraries already provide public Internet access, the library community is well positioned to become community hubs of citizen journalist activity. Unknowingly, or at least unintentionally, many libraries may be serving this role already.

Citizen journalism came to prominence in the aftermath of 9/11 as eyewitness accounts and survival stories, complete with photographs, began appearing on blogs and the Internet. The tsunami disaster elevated citizen journalism into the general consciousness when first-hand survivor videos appeared on the web mere days after the disaster. Citizen journalism further entered the mainstream with the London terrorist bombings of 2005. Within hours of the attack, first-hand mobile phone images were published on blogs and on photo-sharing services like Flickr. The next day, these images appeared in daily newspapers and television newscasts around the world. Hurricane Katrina further showcased the power of citizen journalism. While mainstream media, cut off by the devastation of the flooding, struggled to cover the unfolding story in downtown New Orleans, a blogger bunkered down in a New Orleans data centre continued to publish first-hand accounts, photographs and live webcam images throughout the harrowing days following the storm.[4]

IMPORTANT VOICES

Citizen journalism has not gone unnoticed by the corporate media. Recognizing the value of such reporting, they embrace citizen journalism by integrating it into their print and television programming. *The Washington Post* embeds live Technorati updates for each of its stories, providing readers with real-time feedback and reaction from the web community. CNN television has an "Internet Reporter" who monitors citizen journalist blogs in order to identify and analyze the trends in blogger discussion.[5] Within the last year, both Yahoo and Google have launched blog search engines. Notably, Google has also chosen to incorporate blog posts into its Google News service to further supplement the more mainstream news channels indexed by the site. Many news services actively solicit readers to submit citizen journalism content. After the recent fires at the Buncefield oil depot near London, the BBC was inundated with over 6,500 photographs and videos courtesy of those within eyeshot of the accident.[6]

Closer to home, the 2006 federal election provides an excellent example of the power of citizen journalism. On December 22, 2005, University of Ottawa law professor Michael Geist posted to his blog news of a planned fundraiser for Toronto-area MP Sam Bulte—an event sponsored by several leaders of the Canadian entertainment industry. Geist states in his post, "At $250.00 a person, I have my doubts that many of the artists that Ms. Bulte claims to represent will be present. Instead, it will [sic] lobbyists and lobby groups, eagerly handing over their money with the expectation that the real value of the evening will come long after Margo Timmins has finished her set."[7] On January 1, 2006, the story was mentioned in the widely read Boing Boing blog.[8] Within weeks of this post, *The Globe and Mail*, *National Post*, *Toronto Star* and *Macleans* all published stories mentioning the potential conflict of interest issue raised by Geist. Would this story have been included in these publications without the attention it first received from the blogging world? In the end, Sam Bulte lost her seat in the election. Perhaps the blog world played a role—we can only speculate. But as Michael Geist writes, "Examining the role of blogs is unquestionably interesting and important. It is difficult to quantify, but I'm fairly confident that the online community had a real impact in Parkdale-High Park."[9]

Given the importance of these new voices, what should be the response of the library community to citizen journalism? How can we ensure that the users of our libraries hear these important voices? Do we even have a role in supporting citizen journalism? Navigating and tackling the issues of the loosely structured world of citizen journalism can seem like a daunting task. However, there are a number of steps one can take to integrate citizen journalism into library services and collections. For starters:

- Become familiar with blog aggregation and search tools such as Technorati or the blog search engines of Yahoo and Google. The Technorati front page quickly provides an immediate and current snapshot of the hot topics and stories being discussed in the blogosphere. Wikipedia is also a useful place to observe first-hand citizen journalism activities, especially with emerging news stories. Next time a big world event occurs, test how long it takes for blogs, Flickr or a Wikipedia entry to be created. Consider using RSS or other web-based tools to push news out to your local community.
- Make your library a hub for citizen journalism. Make the citizen journalist toolkit easy to access and use from your library. Promote the use of blogs and other social software on your library website. Develop programming to expose your local community to the world of citizen journalism. Host

a blog that can aggregate different citizen journalist voices from within your local area and help to build an online community with roots in your library.

- Consider expanding your information literacy programming to incorporate media literacy concepts. Citizen journalism means *more voices* and *more diversity*. As a result, media literacy may be even more complex now than it was in the past.

The citizen journalist and the larger blogging community fill an important role in our democracy. The blogosphere is the ultimate accountability check for the actions of governments and corporations. The citizen journalist is at the forefront of this new transparency. Libraries have an opportunity to play a vital role in this equation by supporting citizen journalism within our local communities.

FOOTNOTES

1. "Urban Conflict," *Toronto Star*, Jan. 31, 2006, p. A1.

2. Chris Willis and Shayne Bowman, *We Media: How Audiences Are Shaping the Future of News and Information*, Sept. 3, 2003, www.hypergene.net/wemedia/weblog.php.

3. www.flickr.com/groups/74918957@N00/pool/

4. http://mgno.com

5. www.cnn.com/CNN/anchors_reporters/tatton.abbi.html

6. http://news.bbc.co.uk/1/hi/technology/4566712.stm

7. Michael Geist, *That's What Friends Are For*, Dec. 11, 2005, http://michaelgeist.ca/component/option.com_content/task,view/id,10 47/Itemid,89/.

8. www.boingboing.net/2006/01/01bulte_canadian_mp_ge.html

9. Michael Geist, *Lessons Learned*, Jan. 24, 2006, http://michaelgeist.ca/index.php?option-com_content&task=view&id=1086&Itemid=85.

2

The Newspaper Crisis:
Print Media in the Crosshairs

Editor's Introduction

The past few years have not been kind to the newspaper. In February 2009, Denver, Colorado's *Rocky Mountain News* ceased operations, ending an illustrious history spanning nearly 150 years. The following month, the *Seattle Post-Intelligencer* announced that it would no longer publish a print edition but would continue as an online-only publication. The demise of two major dailies in the space of a month was only the tip of the iceberg, however. Newspapers throughout the country have been downsizing, cutting their staffs through layoffs, attrition, buyouts, or early retirement. Overseas bureaus have been shuttered and the number of people out in the field covering the news has fallen precipitously.

The culprits in the newspaper's decline are not hard to find. For revenue newspapers have long depended on advertising, both classified and otherwise; subscriptions; and newsstand sales. The Internet has essentially eviscerated these revenue streams. Such Web sites as Craigslist.org have rendered traditional classified newspaper ads obsolete. Meanwhile, there is little incentive for readers to subscribe or purchase a newspaper because most content can be accessed on-line for free. Today, anyone with an Internet connection can read *The New York Times*, *The Washington Post*, and thousands of other newspapers, without paying a cent.

Nevertheless, despite these structural impediments, most newspapers have continued to turn a profit, albeit with fewer staffers and declining coverage areas. Still, the rate of return on investment is not high enough to satisfy Wall Street. So the newspaper's downward spiral continues.

The solution to the newspaper's woes is widely acknowledged and seems, on first glance, to be fairly simple. In order to survive, newspapers will have to find a way to generate revenue from their Internet traffic: they need to charge readers to access their material on-line. Simple enough. Yet implementing such a strategy has proven problematic.

The articles in this chapter consider the plight of the newspaper industry and what can be done to arrest its recent slump. Walter Isaacson, in "How to Save Your Newspaper," offers a broad look at the prevailing trends in the newspaper business and proposes the obvious remedy: that newspapers "[get] paid by users for the services they provide and the journalism they produce." Michael Kinsley, in a tongue-in-cheek piece, "Extra! Extra! The Future of Newspapers," describes the evolving manner in which people have consumed newspaper content over the years.

For those employed in the newspaper business, recent years have been harsh. With little job security and the constant fear of the next round of layoffs, morale is tough to keep up. Yet many choose to stay in the field simply because they love the work. In "Hunkering Down," Beth Macy discusses how various journalists are coping with the industry's changing fortunes. For some, the decision to "hunker down" is strangely liberating. As Joe Grimm informed Macy, "Sometimes you might feel like you're being naive, but there's a certain relief that comes when you decide to stick with it and tell yourself: 'I'm tired of being uncertain; I'm staying put.' That's when people start sleeping again."

In "Is There Life after Newspapers?" Robert Hodierne catches up with some casualties of the news business to see how they've adjusted to the next phase of their professional lives. Most have entered other careers, but the transition has not always been an easy one. Yet many don't miss the stress and uncertainty, not to mention the constant deadlines and fast pace. One subject tells Hodierne, "My blood pressure is at least 20 points better than when I was in the newsroom," adding, "Getting laid off six years ago was the best thing that ever happened to me."

While the decline of newspapers has been hard on journalists, it also has ramifications for the public and for democracy. Robin Peek, in "When a Newspaper Falls in the Forest," explores some of these issues, posing the question, "what will fill the void in a community when the unifying fabric of a newspaper is gone?"

Finally, in "Self-Inflicted Wounds," John Morton considers one aspect of the newspaper crisis: the decline in the "standing" of newspapers. "Standing," Morton explains, "encompasses many things: prevalence, respect, influence, personality, reputation and, most of all, relevance." Given the distaste and distrust with which the mainstream media is perceived by large sectors of the public today, it is not surprising that newspapers should come in for a share of criticism as well. However, with fewer people paying for their content, not to mention constant stories about the decline of the industry, newspapers have endured a particularly brutal fall.

How to Save Your Newspaper[*]

By Walter Isaacson
Time, February 5, 2009

During the past few months, the crisis in journalism has reached meltdown proportions. It is now possible to contemplate a time when some major cities will no longer have a newspaper and when magazines and network-news operations will employ no more than a handful of reporters.

There is, however, a striking and somewhat odd fact about this crisis. Newspapers have more readers than ever. Their content, as well as that of newsmagazines and other producers of traditional journalism, is more popular than ever—even (in fact, especially) among young people.

The problem is that fewer of these consumers are paying. Instead, news organizations are merrily giving away their news. According to a Pew Research Center study, a tipping point occurred last year: more people in the U.S. got their news online for free than paid for it by buying newspapers and magazines. Who can blame them? Even an old print junkie like me has quit subscribing to the *New York Times*, because if it doesn't see fit to charge for its content, I'd feel like a fool paying for it.

This is not a business model that makes sense. Perhaps it appeared to when Web advertising was booming and every half-sentient publisher could pretend to be among the clan who "got it" by chanting the mantra that the ad-supported Web was "the future." But when Web advertising declined in the fourth quarter of 2008, free felt like the future of journalism only in the sense that a steep cliff is the future for a herd of lemmings.

Newspapers and magazines traditionally have had three revenue sources: newsstand sales, subscriptions and advertising. The new business model relies only on the last of these. That makes for a wobbly stool even when the one leg is strong. When it weakens—as countless publishers have seen happen as a result of the recession—the stool can't possibly stand.

Henry Luce, a co-founder of *Time*, disdained the notion of giveaway publications that relied solely on ad revenue. He called that formula "morally abhorrent" and also "economically self-defeating." That was because he believed that good journalism required that a publication's primary duty be to its readers, not to its advertisers. In an advertising-only revenue model, the incentive is perverse. It is also self-defeating, because eventually you will weaken your bond with your readers if you do not feel directly dependent on them for your revenue. When a man knows he is to be hanged in a fortnight, Dr. Johnson said, it concentrates his mind wonderfully. Journalism's fortnight is upon us, and I suspect that 2009 will be remembered as the year news organizations realized that further rounds of cost-cutting would not stave off the hangman.

One option for survival being tried by some publications, such as the *Christian Science Monitor* and the *Detroit Free Press*, is to eliminate or drastically cut their print editions and focus on their free websites. Others may try to ride out the long winter, hope that their competitors die and pray that they will grab a large enough share of advertising to make a profitable go of it as free sites. That's fine. We need a variety of competing strategies.

These approaches, however, still make a publication completely beholden to its advertisers. So I am hoping that this year will see the dawn of a bold, old idea that will provide yet another option that some news organizations might choose: getting paid by users for the services they provide and the journalism they produce.

This notion of charging for content is an old idea not simply because newspapers and magazines have been doing it for more than four centuries. It's also something they used to do at the dawn of the online era, in the early 1990s. Back then there were a passel of online service companies, such as Prodigy, CompuServe, Delphi and AOL. They used to charge users for the minutes people spent online, and it was naturally in their interest to keep the users online for as long as possible. As a result, good content was valued. When I was in charge of *Time*'s nascent online-media department back then, every year or so we would play off AOL and CompuServe; one year the bidding for our magazine and bulletin boards reached $1 million.

Then along came tools that made it easier for publications and users to venture onto the open Internet rather than remain in the walled gardens created by the online services. I remember talking to Louis Rossetto, then the editor of *Wired*, about ways to put our magazines directly online, and we decided that the best strategy was to use the hypertext markup language and transfer protocols that defined the World Wide Web. *Wired* and *Time* made the plunge the same week in 1994, and within a year most other publications had done so as well. We invented things like banner ads that brought in a rising tide of revenue, but the upshot was that we abandoned getting paid for content.

One of history's ironies is that hypertext—an embedded Web link that refers you to another page or site—had been invented by Ted Nelson in the early 1960s with the goal of enabling micropayments for content. He wanted to make sure that the people who created good stuff got rewarded for it. In his vision, all links on a page would facilitate the accrual of small, automatic payments for whatever content was accessed. Instead, the Web got caught up in the ethos that information wants to be free. Others smarter than we were had avoided that trap. For example, when Bill Gates noticed in 1976 that hobbyists were freely sharing Altair BASIC, a code he and his colleagues had written, he sent an open letter to members of the Homebrew Computer Club telling them to stop. "One thing you do is prevent good software from being written," he railed. "Who can afford to do professional work for nothing?"

The easy Internet ad dollars of the late 1990s enticed newspapers and magazines to put all of their content, plus a whole lot of blogs and whistles, onto their websites for free. But the bulk of the ad dollars has ended up flowing to groups that did not actually create much content but instead piggybacked on it: search engines, portals and some aggregators.

Another group that benefits from free journalism is Internet service providers. They get to charge customers $20 to $30 a month for access to the Web's trove of free content and services. As a result, it is not in their interest to facilitate easy ways for media creators to charge for their content. Thus we have a world in which phone companies have accustomed kids to paying up to 20 cents when they send a text message but it seems technologically and psychologically impossible to get people to pay 10 cents for a magazine, newspaper or newscast.

Currently a few newspapers, most notably the *Wall Street Journal,* charge for their online editions by requiring a monthly subscription. When Rupert Murdoch acquired the *Journal,* he ruminated publicly about dropping the fee. But Murdoch is, above all, a smart businessman. He took a look at the economics and decided it was lunacy to forgo the revenue—and that was even before the online ad market began contracting. Now his move looks really smart. Paid subscriptions for the *Journal's* website were up more than 7% in a very gloomy 2008. Plus, he spooked the *New York Times* into dropping its own halfhearted attempts to get subscription revenue, which were based on the (I think flawed) premise that it should charge for the paper's punditry rather than for its great reporting. (*Author's note: After publication the* New York *Times vehemently denied that their thinking was influenced by outside considerations; I accept their explanation.*)

But I don't think that subscriptions will solve everything—nor should they be the only way to charge for content. A person who wants one day's edition of a newspaper or is enticed by a link to an interesting article is rarely going to go through the cost and hassle of signing up for a subscription under today's clunky payment systems. The key to attracting online revenue, I think, is to come up with an iTunes-easy method of micropayment. We need something like digital coins or an E-ZPass digital wallet—a one-click system with a really simple interface that will permit impulse purchases of a newspaper, magazine, article, blog or video for a penny, nickel, dime or whatever the creator chooses to charge.

Admittedly, the Internet is littered with failed micropayment companies. If you remember Flooz, Beenz, CyberCash, Bitpass, Peppercoin and DigiCash, it's probably because you lost money investing in them. Many tracts and blog entries have been written about how the concept can't work because of bad tech or mental transaction costs.

But things have changed. "With newspapers entering bankruptcy even as their audience grows, the threat is not just to the companies that own them, but also to the news itself," wrote the savvy New York *Times* columnist David Carr last month in a column endorsing the idea of paid content. This creates a necessity that ought to be the mother of invention. In addition, our two most creative digital innovators have shown that a pay-per-drink model can work when it's made easy enough: Steve Jobs got music consumers (of all people) comfortable with the concept of paying 99 cents for a tune instead of Napsterizing an entire industry, and Jeff Bezos with his Kindle showed that consumers would buy electronic versions of books, magazines and newspapers if purchases could be done simply.

What Internet payment options are there today? PayPal is the most famous, but it has transaction costs too high for impulse buys of less than a dollar. The denizens of Facebook are embracing systems like Spare Change, which allows them to charge their PayPal accounts or credit cards to get digital currency they can spend in small amounts. Similar services include Bee-Tokens and Tipjoy. Twitter users have Twitpay, which is a micropayment service for the micromessaging set. Gamers have their own digital currencies that can be used for impulse buys during online role-playing games. And real-world commuters are used to gizmos like E-ZPass, which deducts automatically from their prepaid account as they glide through a highway tollbooth.

Under a micropayment system, a newspaper might decide to charge a nickel for an article or a dime for that day's full edition or $2 for a month's worth of Web access. Some surfers would balk, but I suspect most would merrily click through if it were cheap and easy enough.

The system could be used for all forms of media: magazines and blogs, games and apps, TV newscasts and amateur videos, porn pictures and policy monographs, the reports of citizen journalists, recipes of great cooks and songs of garage bands. This would not only offer a lifeline to traditional media outlets but also nourish citizen journalists and bloggers. They have vastly enriched our realms of information and ideas, but most can't make much money at it. As a result, they tend to do it for the ego kick or as a civic contribution. A micropayment system would allow regular folks, the types who have to worry about feeding their families, to supplement their income by doing citizen journalism that is of value to their community.

When I used to go fishing in the bayous of Louisiana as a boy, my friend Thomas would sometimes steal ice from those machines outside gas stations. He had the theory that ice should be free. We didn't reflect much on who would make the ice if it were free, but fortunately we grew out of that phase. Likewise, those who believe that all content should be free should reflect on who will open bureaus in Baghdad or be able to fly off as freelancers to report in Rwanda under such a system.

I say this not because I am "evil," which is the description my daughter slings at those who want to charge for their Web content, music or apps. Instead, I say this because my daughter is very creative, and when she gets older, I want her to get paid for producing really neat stuff rather than come to me for money or decide that it makes more sense to be an investment banker.

I say this, too, because I love journalism. I think it is valuable and should be valued by its consumers. Charging for content forces discipline on journalists: they must produce things that people actually value. I suspect we will find that this necessity is actually liberating. The need to be valued by readers—serving them first and foremost rather than relying solely on advertising revenue—will allow the media once again to set their compass true to what journalism should always be about.

Extra! Extra!*

The Future of Newspapers

By Michael Kinsley
Slate, January 7, 2006

Somewhere in the forest, a tree is cut down. It is loaded onto a giant truck and hauled a vast distance to a factory, where the trees are turned into huge rolls of paper. These rolls are loaded onto another truck and hauled another vast distance to another factory, where the rolls of paper are covered in ink, chopped up, folded, stacked, tied, and loaded onto a third set of trucks, which fan out across cities and regions dropping bundles here and there.

Printing plants no longer have the clickety-clack of linotype machines and bubbling vats of molten lead. The letterpress machines that stamped the ink on the paper have been supplanted by offset presses that transfer it gently. There is computer-controlled this and that. Nevertheless, the process remains highly physical, mechanical, complicated, and noisy. As we live through the second industrial revolution, your daily newspaper remains a tribute to the wonders of the first one.

Meanwhile, back to those bundles. Some of them are opened and the newspapers are put, one-by-one, into plastic bags. Bagged or unbagged, they are loaded onto a fourth set of vehicles—bicycles by legend, usually these days a car or small truck—and flung individually into your bushes or at your cat. Other bundles go to retail establishments. Still other newspapers are locked into attractive metal boxes bolted into the sidewalk. Anyone who is feeling lucky and happens to possess the exact change has a decent shot at obtaining a paper or, for the same price, carting away a dozen.

What happens next is aided by a flat surface, especially on a Sunday near Christmas. The proud owner of up to four or five pounds of paper and ink begins searching for the parts he or she wants. The paper has multiple sections, each of which is either folded into others or wrapped around others according to an ancient formula known only to newspaper publishers and designed to guarantee that no one section can either be found on the first go-through or removed without putting half a dozen other sections into play. Newspaper-industry regulations do not require any particular labeling system for sections, but they do require that if letters are used, the sections cannot be in alphabetical order.

And so, at last, there are two piles of paper: a short one of stuff to read, and a tall one of stuff to throw away. Unfortunately, many people are taking the logic of this process one step further. Instead of buying a paper in order to throw most of it away, they are not buying it in the first place.

Bill Gates says that in technology things that are supposed to happen in less than five years usually take longer than expected, while things that are supposed to happen in more than 10 years usually come sooner than expected. Ten years ago, when I went to work for Microsoft, the newspaper industry was in a panic over something called Sidewalk—a now-forgotten Microsoft project to create Web site entertainment guides for a couple dozen big cities. Newspapers were convinced that Microsoft could and would put them out of business by stealing their ad base. It didn't happen. The collapse of the Internet bubble did happen. And, until very recently, the newspapers got complacent. Some developed good Web sites, some didn't, but most stopped thinking of the Web as an imminent danger.

Ten years later, newspapers are starting to panic again. But merely slobbering after bloggers may not be enough. In 1996, the oldest Americans who grew up with computers and don't even understand my tiresome anecdotes about how people used to resist them ("What's a typewriter, Mike?") were just entering adulthood. Now they are most of the working population, or close to it.

The trouble even an established customer will take to obtain a newspaper continues to shrink, as well. Once, I would drive across town if necessary. Today, I open the front door and if the paper isn't within about 10 feet I retreat to my computer and read it online. Only six months ago, that figure was 20 feet. Extrapolating, they will have to bring it to me in bed by the end of the year and read it to me out loud by the second quarter of 2007.

No one knows how all this will play out. But it is hard to believe that there will be room in the economy for delivering news by the Rube Goldberg process described above. That doesn't mean newspapers are toast. After all, they've got the brand names. You gotta trust something called the "Post-Intelligencer" more than something called "Yahoo!" or "Google," don't you? No, seriously, don't you? OK, how old did you say you are?

And newspapers have got the content. The first time I heard myself called a "content provider," I felt like a guy who'd been hired by the company that makes Tupperware to make sure there was plenty of Jell-O salad. As a rule, anyone who uses the term "content provider" without a smirk needs to consider getting content from someone else.

There is even hope for newspapers in the very absurdity of their current methods of production and distribution. What customers pay for a newspaper doesn't cover the cost of the paper, let alone the attendant folderol. Without these costs, even zero revenue from customers would be a good deal for newspapers, if adver-tisers go along. Which they might. Maybe. Don't you think? Please?

Hunkering Down[*]

By Beth Macy
American Journalism Review, June/July 2009

There are days when I dream about quitting the newspaper business and opening my own coffee shop. I'd call it the Underdog Café. On rainy days, the lunch special would be tomato pie and biscuits. My lovable but dumb dog, Lucky, would bask in a pool of front-window light. Customers would feel so at home at the Underdog that sometimes—but not too often—they would forget to pay.

But the daydream always ends there, before the dinner menu is even sketched out.

After 23 years in the business, after seeing my white-haired brethren grudgingly accept buyouts, after the uncertainty of watching the corporate execs put our newspaper on the market—only to take it off when the economy tanked—not only am I still here at the *Roanoke Times*, but I still get excited when I happen onto a great story. That's why I stick with journalism, even as it threatens to bail on me.

Call me a Pollyanna; some of my favorite coworkers do. But there's a certain relief that came when I decided earlier this year to plant my entire body in the sand, Reporter's Notebook and all. I don't like the presses shutting down in Denver and Seattle. I hate the fact that thousands of American journalists have lost their jobs to buyouts and layoffs already this year, and many others have made the preemptive move of getting out before they're forced out.

But more than 40,000 newspaper journalists are still cranking away, and I'm grateful to be among them, having vowed to ride out the tsunami until they pry the company-owned laptop from my cold, ink-stained hands.

As Poynter Online recruiting columnist and former *Detroit Free Press* recruiter Joe Grimm puts it, "Sometimes you might feel like you're being naive, but there's a certain relief that comes when you decide to stick with it and tell yourself: 'I'm tired of being uncertain; I'm staying put.' That's when people start sleeping again."

I've spent evenings, weekends and furlough days for the past few months talking to some of the hardy sleepers among us, sussing out the best psychological strategies for staying sane while staying put. Sometimes, the conversations buoyed my resolve; other times, they gave me heart palpitations.

A few journalists I contacted were so distraught they couldn't talk. Others obliged, but I had to employ my typing shorthand to deal with their rapid shifts between on and off the record because they were nervous about their editors' reactions to the story.

Reporter Lindsay Peterson says the discussion brought therapeutic relief. "It's like when your boyfriend breaks up with you, and you quit going out," she wrote after our talk, "and then a friend of his calls, and you spend three hours talking about him and whether you'll ever get back together again."

Amy Ellis Nutt sees herself as a kind of midwife. A national award-winning enterprise reporter for Newark's *Star-Ledger*, Nutt believes she's witnessing the rebirth of journalism from a bedside seat, trying to manage the labor pains and hoping that, whatever happens, there will always be a way for her to tell stories and make the public's business known.

But, as any postpartum mom will tell you, the roughest part of labor is the time between the contractions; the uncertainty of not knowing when the next painful swell is coming and whether it will hurt more than the last.

Nutt was present at the end of 2008 when the Newhouse-owned paper lost 46 percent of its editorial staff. The farewells and obligatory cakes were staggered, with nearly half of the 150 staffers leaving on December 31. The grief was monolithic.

"It's sad to see so many good people falling away from the profession and so much institutional memory lost," she says. "Some days you feel like you're slowly being buried up to your neck, but you're still there, still breathing."

Journalists who cope best focus on what lured them into the business to start with, Nutt believes. "Journalism is needed now more than ever, from the smallest profiles of ordinary people to the investigations of where the bailout money is going."

This year, Nutt has investigated living kidney donations and the effects of reduced public funding on people with disabilities. "And you hear from people, and they thank you for listening to them and trying to tell their stories. And those are the things that never change. So you psych yourself up, because there are fewer people telling these stories, which means there are even more reasons for you to get out there and do them."

Because Nutt came to the profession later than most—at 54, she's worked for newspapers for 12 years—she retains an enthusiasm unusual for many staffers her age. She's perhaps also more apt to embrace collaboration with photographers, videographers and online producers, as journalists of all stripes try to build the medium of the future.

Nutt co-writes narration for video scripts that accompany her stories, reports and posts stories online for the paper's continuous news desk and tries to learn online skills from much younger staffers. While she's always working on at least one enterprise project, she likes to simultaneously tackle short-range stories, too.

"I know great reporters who just don't see themselves moving into the next phase of the business. But I'm not someone who only wants to work on projects; I like working on deadline. I'll pitch in and take dictation for someone in the field. I still love the excitement of being in a newsroom, and I don't mind having to learn new things."

Amid the shrunken newsroom at the *Star-Ledger*, a complicated camaraderie, borne of relief, survivor's guilt and excitement for the future, has emerged, she says. "We're starting over, and there is not quite optimism, but at least a sense of curiosity about what's going to happen."

"We're the ones left in the lifeboat. We made it off the ship, and we're out in the big ocean. But we're alive, and we're together, and one way or another, we are going to get to shore."

Already, Bill Reiter can hear his colleagues at McClatchy's *Kansas City Star* laughing. His buddies from J-school, too, the ones who call him when they're feeling nervous about the state of the industry.

In the testosterone temple that is the American newsroom, Reiter knows he'll be teased for his unbridled optimism, his belief that journalism's glass is still half full. "I feel like I live in Middle Earth, and the dark cloud has covered the land," Reiter says.

What right does he have to be so happy about his job? After all, he's a mortgageholder with a journalist-wife and a kid on the way, and he works as a sports enterprise reporter at a paper that has had four rounds of layoffs, saying goodbye to more than 100 staffers.

There's plenty to do at work; he feels lucky to get to write Sunday takeouts on a near-weekly basis. But he also spends half his free time "trying to talk fellow journalists off the ledge."

Here's what he tells them: "I can't save the newspaper industry, and I can't stop layoffs, and I can't impact the recession. I know this is a cliché, but I can only do the best work that I can do, and I happen to still love it. If you still love it, love it while you can." Besides, in this economy, no profession is layoff-proof.

Reiter, 31, believes journalists are craving colleagues and editors who inspire them, who trust them and who know that the key to rowing through the rocky shoals of reinvention is telling great stories.

"Everywhere I look there are signs that people are desperate to feel good about journalism," he says. The Web site sportsjournalists.com—where sports reporters typically complain about the uselessness of awards—took an uncharacteristic turn as participants urged the complainers to "be quiet; give us something to celebrate, for once!" Reiter recalls.

His buddy Reid Forgrave noticed the same response at a beer-and-bitch session following the latest Iowa Newspaper Association awards dinner. Forgrave, a reporter for Gannett's *Des Moines Register*, says the usual complaints about "my editor wouldn't let me write a 40-inch story; it had to be 25" were gone.

"The old complaints almost seem like a luxury now," says Forgrave, 30. Even with the announcements of Gannett-wide furloughs, "People weren't too happy about sacrificing a week's pay, but they weren't as irate as you might expect. It was more like, 'At least we're not getting laid off.'"

What keeps him going is the readers who are desperate to tell their stories. The day before his weeklong furlough was to begin in February, a source tipped him off to a 70-year-old woman being kicked out of her house because it was in foreclosure—even though she'd paid her rent.

"Those are the stories that I'm most scared of losing. You can always say foreclosures are up 4.2 percent, but when you show it happening to an old woman who's on her front lawn with her granddaughters going through her stuff . . ."

Even though he can't always do it, Forgrave knows he does better work when he protects himself from newsroom negativity, even if it means trying to distance himself from some coworkers and the poisonous drumbeat of Romenesko postings. It would help, he adds, if more editors across the country doled out "honest, positive encouragement that plays to our conscience, to our calling—the reason we got into the business in the first place," Forgrave says.

He likes to take the long view, imagining the industry five or 10 years into the future: "We've figured out how to make money on the Web and we're back to the place where we're not all Chicken Little anymore."

"It will probably have been good for us to have had the spotlight shone on us. For once, we'll feel more in tune with the people we're covering . . . down to the level of what newspaper writers used to be and back to the people that we should be writing about more—the voiceless."

Investigative reporter Lindsay Peterson is planning for her journalistic day of reckoning—sort of. Her paper, Media General's *Tampa Tribune*, has had so many rounds of buyouts she can't keep the number straight, and the reporting staff is now roughly half the size it was when she arrived there two decades ago. Fierce competition with the *St. Petersburg Times* has many reporters in the region wondering which paper will be the last one standing.

Still, Peterson decided a long time ago: If the ship's sinking, she's going down with it. "I really didn't think the ship was going to go down when I first said it, but right now everybody's looking for a lifeboat. The problem is, those lifeboats aren't very sturdy. The friends who've gone into PR jobs, it's OK; it's a paycheck. But if they could turn the clock back, they would come back."

Peterson, 53, says most of her peers are riding out the storm, or trying to. "The only way I know how to do it is just to keep looking for that next story," she says.

She's caught, though, between not knowing which stories appeal most to Web users (and the advertisers who court them) and feeling guilty about not putting print loyalists first. She frequently questions whether she's putting her energy into the right stories, trying to divine what it is people want to read on the Internet. "The stories we put our hearts and souls into don't seem to be getting as many hits as we'd hoped," she says.

A recent narrative she wrote about a wounded soldier from Iraq garnered 6,000 hits—and only slowly, over several weeks of traveling around the Internet—while a colleague's salacious news story about a teacher caught sleeping with a student generated far more page views and comments.

Earlier this year, a series of articles about an eccentric woman traveling from Florida to Texas on horseback surprised her by scratching her writing itch—and attracting a huge Internet following across the country, becoming the paper's most e-mailed story the day it ran.

"I had a great time with it because, finally, it met all the criteria, and the editors were drooling," she says. "But I don't think they expected it, either. You might think a story is interesting or you may not, but it's like the viewers are the ones deciding now."

"It's more democratic, yes, and it's something we need to pay attention to. But it's disturbing and disruptive, too."

Peterson hopes the value of journalism will somehow endure in the media-reinvention process, and by some miracle she will be able to outlast the coming changes. Plan B, though, if she does get laid off, is to get her doctoral degree in journalism, using the demise of newspapers as her thesis topic.

"I want to understand it," she says. "The only thing that keeps me from getting depressed is that I just can't comprehend what's happening; that we're all looking at possibly losing our jobs . . . It's still just unbelievable."

Dan Suwyn has advice for Peterson and all the other realists out there. And for their bosses. A former journalist who now runs a change-management consultancy called the Rapid Change Group, Suwyn, 45, says layoffs not only affect the mental health of the survivors left behind; they also have an impact on productivity. If the normal worker is productive five out of eight hours in the day, for a worker in the aftermath of a layoff or buyout that number plummets to 1.5 to 1.8 hours a day, he says, citing government statistics. He says that effect can last anywhere from three weeks to a year, depending on the magnitude of the cuts.

Journalists are obsessing: How are we going to do more work with fewer workers? Did I make a mistake by staying? Do I need to get out, too?

"Most managers don't know how to deal with people who are angry, but people who are angry are still demonstrating that they care, and that's a good thing," he says.

While reporters are still in the caring mode, editors should set transparent and specific goals—for example, to increase page views for stories, develop more interactive ways to pull in readers, make city government coverage more relevant—and then celebrate every tiny victory along the way. "Right now," Suwyn says, "what I see most media companies doing is kicking into survival mode instead of into, 'How do we show the employees who are left that they're safe and respected? That they have a chance to contribute to this so they can use their intelligence to help grow the media company of the future?'"

Journalists need to realize that if they're not already working in a free-agent economy, they soon could be, Suwyn says. "Ask yourself: 'How do the skills and principles I have apply to different media? What can I do better online?' Maybe you get to be the last person to turn out the [newsroom] lights, and that's great. But in case you're not, think about how you can apply your principles in a different medium."

"Newspapers no longer have the market cornered on journalism, so what are you going to do? It's not just about Budweiser any more. There are lots of microbreweries and, while the microbreweries might not pay as well, sometimes they are more rewarding."

Patrick Evans hopes to continue working for his CBS television affiliate, KPSP in Palm Springs, California, for the rest of his career. While his station has so far been spared layoffs, many of his broadcasting peers who work elsewhere have been asked to take a pay cut—or to take off—a situation that makes contract-renewal time fraught with anxiety for everyone in the field.

"For those of us who have chosen to tough it out, you've got to wake up, get to work, be enthusiastic about what you're doing and make sure your bosses and your viewers know you love being there," the senior meteorologist says. "Because there is always someone younger and cheaper who would love to do your job."

With his wife also in the media industry—Carol Horton is the marketing manager for Palm Springs' *Desert Sun*—the couple thinks it's smart to have an alternate plan that has nothing to do with the media. Evans, 42, has long wanted to open his own restaurant. And while he concedes that being a restaurateur is also a challenge these days, every weekend he tries to perfect at least one dish for his would-be menu.

He's also started taking the Foreign Service Exam on an annual basis. Though no U.S. State Department offers in media relations have emerged, "It's a good mental exercise and, if the opportunity came up, it would be fascinating."

"I don't want to have to leave," he adds. "But I think it's prudent to think about it and be prepared."

Evans stays upbeat by trying to be grateful for family, friends and good health and by finding joy in the work he does. "Today the temperature was 80 and tomorrow it might be 81, and I've got to discern that one degree," he jokes.

Perhaps one of the biggest mysteries about the sinking ship is that there are still young passengers trying to get on board. When American University senior Jill Holbrook declared her communication studies major three years ago, she thought she'd be relying mainly on her story-writing skills. But the 22-year-old has learned to blog, tweet, shoot and edit video, edit sound for radio and—oh yeah—report and write.

She knows how to do a little of everything, but sometimes she frets that she doesn't do any of it very well. Still, she's gotten so good at writing tight for journalism classes that for the first time in her academic career, she struggled to write a 20-page literature paper.

Holbrook was two years into her studies before she became aware that getting a job in an industry that's shifting by the second might be tough. And then the recession hit. "I wish I would have been warned that I was going into a dying industry,"

Holbrook says. "A little heads-up like, 'You probably won't be getting a job when you get out' would have been nice."

On the last day of her college career, she was thrilled to learn she'd landed a part-time job as a board operator for Sirius XM, where she'd been interning. She hopes the position will eventually lead to a full-time job as a radio reporter or producer.

Those rookies lucky enough to find jobs may be replacing some beloved and bought-out colleagues, but veterans would be wise to cozy up to them more than they do now, advises Amy Eisman, Holbrook's writing for convergent media professor and the director of writing programs at American's School of Communication.

Recent college grads "are a great resource, and so are you guys," says Eisman, a founding editor of *USA Today*. "They're just in awe of the veteran journalists, but they don't know how to ask questions as well as you do." Information comes to them so readily online that they're also not as good at judging its credibility, she says.

Eisman worries, though, that her graduates aren't embraced by newsroom long-timers for the "great pile of skills they leave us with" and instead end up shoveling copy from here to there for years, with no opportunity for advancement. "In some places, the industry isn't always caught up with them."

Veterans hoping to become transitional journalists—rather than transitioned journalists—stand to learn a lot from young journalists such as Holbrook, beyond their technical prowess. The newcomers tend to be more comfortable injecting first-person point of views into stories and cultivating niche areas of expertise. They're also more likely to grasp how to brand themselves in the free-agent economy, where reporters don't just write stories for the companies they work for; they also promote their work via their own blogs and through Facebook and Twitter.

"They're being directed by people who are thrilled to have them but don't know how much they know and how much they still need to learn and how much they want to be just like them . . . but with digital skill sets," Eisman says.

The best transitional journalists don't look upon their digital comrades as the younger, cheaper versions of their former colleagues, but as people they can't afford not to learn from. Working together, Eisman predicts, journalists can steer the industry away from the abyss.

"Just like with the economy, I think it's going to get worse," she says, "and then eventually something beautiful is going to grow up from the ashes."

Is There Life After Newspapers?[*]

By Robert Hodierne
American Journalism Review, February/March 2009

Erica Smith has a job as a graphics designer for the *St. Louis Post-Dispatch*. At least for now. There are few journalists in America who know as well as Smith how tenuous a steady newspaper job is these days. For the last year and a half, she has spent 10 or 12 hours a week at an old oak table in her sixth-floor loft with her Mac laptop, a bottle of Pepsi and her cat, tallying the fallen: 18 more jobs cut at the *Tallahassee Democrat*, 15 at the *Desert Sun*, 13 at the *Jackson Sun*. And the list goes on and on. Eight at the Visalia *Times-Delta*, 12 at the *Statesman Journal*, 125 at the *Virginian-Pilot*, 60 at the Asheville *Citizen-Times*.

Smith tallied 15,554 newspaper job cuts for 2008, and she was still updating in January. Her research is artfully rendered on a Web page called "paper cuts" (graphicdesignr.net/paper cuts/) and appears to be the only such comprehensive list.

"I started out because I was curious about the number of cuts. Now it's because I have too many friends who've been laid off," says Smith, 32, who got into the newspaper business right after graduating from Northwest Missouri State University.

Her tally, which she builds from news releases, wire reports, blogs and tips from colleagues, includes all newspaper jobs, not just those in the newsroom. But she estimates half of those 15,000 cuts were journalists. And that means the newsroom population of American papers shrank by about 15 percent last year, down from 52,000 at the start of the year. That's three times larger than the single greatest annual newsroom employment decrease since 1978, when the American Society of Newspaper Editors began making estimates of the editorial workforce.

But it's worse than that. Smith cautions that her count actually understates the total because many newspapers don't announce layoffs. What's more, her total does not include jobs lost through attrition.

The U.S. Bureau of Labor Statistics' count for all newspaper jobs—from reporter to delivery truck driver—shows the payroll shrinking from 336,000 at the start of the year to 313,600 through October, a drop of 22,400 positions.

Smith, a cheerful woman who laughs easily, finds this all a bit depressing. "I can only update so many at a time without wanting to jump off the ninth floor of the building I live in," she says, with not a trace of a laugh. The 2,000 layoffs that Gannett announced during the holiday season did nothing to improve her mood and kept her swamped for a week.

All of which raises a question: What happens to all of those laid-off and bought-out journalists? Is there life after newspapers? To find out, I posted a questionnaire about the fate of those who have lost their newspaper jobs.

A word of caution here: This was not a scientific poll, because there is no comprehensive list of those who've been laid off from which to draw a random sample. Instead, AJR posted a link to the questionnaire on its homepage (ajr.org). I advertised on Journalismjobs.com and posted word on every online venue I could find aimed at journalists, including Jim Romenesko's popular blog on the Poynter Institute Web site (poynter.org).

In the end, 595 people who say they left newspaper editorial jobs in the last decade under circumstances that were not totally voluntary filled out the questionnaire. Since this wasn't a random sample but rather a self-selected group, there's no way to know whether this group accurately represents the entire universe of people who have been forced out of newspapering. But it offers some interesting insights.

Many of the respondents have found new jobs. It's too early to tell about those who lost their jobs within the past year, but for those who did so between 1999 and 2007:

- Just under 36 percent said they found a new job in less than three months. Add those who say they freelance full time, and the total jumps to 53 percent.
- Less than 10 percent say it took them longer than a year.
- Only a handful—6 percent—found other newspaper jobs. The rest are doing everything from public relations to teaching to driving a bus and clerking in a liquor store.

While they've found work, many of the people with new jobs are making less money. The midpoint salary range for their old jobs was $50,000 to $59,000. Those who listed salaries for their new jobs were a full salary band lower—$40,000 to $49,000.

Of the people who volunteered their old newspaper salary, only 2 percent made less than $20,000 a year. Of the people who gave me their new salaries, that number shot up to 17 percent. The age of those at the bottom of the salary scale has changed surprisingly as well. The median age of those who made less than $20,000 at their old newspaper job was 24. The median age of those now making less than $20,000 is 48.

Here's another surprise: While the overwhelming majority—85 percent—say they miss working at a paper, they are often happier in their new jobs. Sixty-two percent tell us they had been satisfied in their old newspaper jobs; 78 percent report being satisfied in their new jobs. (The bus driver and liquor store clerk are not finding much job satisfaction, however.)

So it's safe to say there is life after newspapers. But it's not always the life the journalists had expected.

Take, for instance, Theresa Conroy.

Conroy, 46, wanted to be a reporter from the get-go. "At 12 years old I can remember saying to my mother that I wanted to be a newspaper reporter," she says. "I was nosy, and I always wanted to know everything first."

Conroy estimates that 90 percent of the journalists of her generation felt the same way she did about the field: "I don't think I ever considered anything else."

For the last five years of her career, Conroy covered cops and criminal courts for the *Philadelphia Daily News*, inevitably described as a scrappy tabloid living in the shadow of its larger sibling, the *Inquirer*. In all, she worked 12 years at the *Daily News*. A former Knight Ridder paper, the *Daily News*, along with the *Inquirer*, was purchased by a group of local investors in 2006.

Conroy says her stint at the paper was great fun—the colorful characters, the scoops, the deadline pressure, the colleagues. But toward the end, with a shrinking staff and a shrinking paper, "most of the time we felt beaten down," she says.

"I was profoundly heartbroken by journalism," she says. "It became less and less, and I started to love it less and less."

To deal with the stress in her life and to help her quit smoking, Conroy took up yoga. She became a part-time yoga instructor, shaking the "stink off" from her grim day job by teaching clients how to relax.

In January 2007, Conroy volunteered to be laid off; she took the 31 weeks of pay and walked away. For the past nine months she's had her own yoga studio in Philadelphia's Roxborough section called Yoga on the Ridge, and she's "doing pretty well." She says the satisfaction she got from breaking a big story isn't nearly as great as the satisfaction she gets now helping an elderly patient with Parkinson's disease do something simple, like stand up.

But, she adds, "I can't quite shake the crime reporter persona. I may be the only yoga teacher who says 'f***' in class."

As for journalism, she says, "I have to say, overwhelmingly and surprisingly, I don't miss it. . . . I'm very happy at what I'm doing."

But for every Conroy, who doesn't miss it and has found meaningful work, there is a Joseph Demma. Demma, 65, is purely old school in the tough-talking, hard-living New York tradition.

"I first wanted to be a reporter in high school," he says. "I watched a TV show called 'Night Beat.' There was a reporter who'd sit over his typewriter with a fedora hat and a cigarette in his mouth, and he'd go around helping people by writing about them."

DAILY NEWSPAPER EDITORIAL WORKFORCE

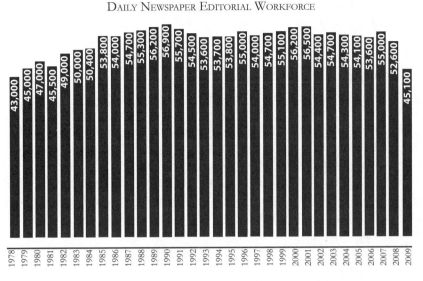

Source: ASNE diversity study
"Based on an estimate of last year's cut by Erica Smith, who maintains the Web page 'paper cuts'"

Demma started as a copy boy at *Newsday* in 1965. He had a good run. He ended up working on the investigative team run by the legendary Bob Greene, who gave the young Demma this advice as he went on his first out-of-town trip for *Newsday*: "You're going to be judged by how much money you spend." It was the good old days. Greene wasn't telling Demma to scrimp.

As an investigative reporter and later editor, he had a hand in three Pulitzer Prize-winning projects. But hard living caught up with him, and in 1998 he left Newsday and went to Reno, Nevada, which is not at the top of everyone's list of places to go to straighten out your life. But he did. In Reno he taught at the University of Nevada and did freelance reporting and investigating. After stints in California at papers in Modesto and Sacramento, he moved to Florida to be near his elderly mother. In 2004 he took over as investigative editor of the Tribune Co.-owned *South Florida Sun-Sentinel* in Fort Lauderdale. "FEMA, Legacy of Waste," a series he oversaw, was a Pulitzer finalist in 2006.

Then on July 18, 2008, the day before he was to start vacation, Demma was laid off. Seven weeks' pay, health insurance until October, and that was it. He's been without full-time work ever since.

"It's tough to get a job when you're 65," he says. "And there are fewer and fewer jobs out there."

When he's not riding his silver Yamaha V-Star Silverado motorcycle, he does some part-time investigative work for lawyers. But he'd really like to get some newspaper work; three days a week on a copy desk would be fine. Otherwise, he says, "I may have to become a greeter at Wal-Mart."

But he has no desire to go back to newspapering full time. "If you were to ask me to go back into that pit again, I'd say, 'No thanks,'" he says. "I thank God I'm not 40 years old with two kids in high school that I have to put through college."

On the brighter side, a year ago his heart was in such rotten shape doctors had to put in a stent. Now, he says, "My health has never been better. My blood pressure is down 25 points. I exercise."

Generally, journalists Demma's age have a harder time finding work than their younger colleagues. For those laid off between 1999 and 2007 who responded to the questionnaire, journalists who needed more than a year to find a job averaged 51 years old. Those who found work in less than three months averaged 46.

But try telling that to Chris Jackson.

Jackson, 30, graduated in 2000 from the University of Arizona as a journalism major. After a stint at the Arizona *Daily Star* in Tucson, he took a job at the *Daily Breeze* in Torrance, California. Jackson remembers that February 28, 2008, was an especially busy day, so he was surprised to be called to the paper's human resources office. There he found his editor and the head of HR for the Los Angeles Newspaper Group, which includes the *Daily Breeze*.

"'We're sorry,' they told me," Jackson recalls. He was one of six let go that day, the Leap Year Six, they call themselves. He was given four weeks' pay and health insurance for three months. Jackson went back to work and finished his shift.

When he didn't find work right away, Jackson had to move back in with his parents in Albuquerque. He has applied for sports information jobs at several universities. One person he interviewed with told him, "Frankly, I don't think newspaper people have the skills to do what we do."

Jackson has applied to be a substitute teacher while he figures out "what I want to do."

Another young casualty of the collapse of the American newspaper business is A. Dominic Efferson, 29, a 2007 graduate of Humboldt State University in Arcata, California. He majored in visual journalism, "the journalism of the future," Efferson says.

In January 2008, he got a job at California's *Eureka Reporter*, an upstart daily in a town that already had a daily. For a time, the town of about 26,000 was on the short list of places with two daily newspapers. But it wasn't to last. In November, the paper closed, throwing Efferson and 20 other journalists out of work.

"It had its ups and downs, but I totally loved it," Efferson says. But now he's "kicking the idea around whether I need to be in a newsroom right now. I've been kicking the idea around of joining the Peace Corps.

"I guess," he concludes, "it was the wrong time to get into the newspaper industry."

Sometimes companies that lay people off provide the services of an outplacement firm to help the newly jobless find new work. John Challenger is chief executive officer of Challenger, Gray & Christmas, the oldest outplacement company in the country.

"Everyone hopes there's an agent out there who will find a job for them," Challenger says. "One of the first key hurdles to get over is there is no agent who'll find them a job. They have to find it themselves. . . . The world doesn't call you, you've got to call it."

Not surprisingly, Challenger points journalists toward jobs that require strong writing skills. "Journalists are good at writing," he says. "That might mean writing books, it might mean writing for company publications of one kind or another, it might be communications more broadly—marketing communications." He also thinks journalists are "generally more intellectual" than most people. That's on the plus side. The downside Challenger sees in journalists is "a lot of time journalists are more internally focused." He tells clients to "connect with lots and lots of your brethren, because the best way to find a new position is to follow your compatriots to their places." And get out in the community. "Go to lunches," he says.

Challenger advises out-of-work newspaper people to "get a fast start. Don't think about it too long. A lot of people spend a lot of time thinking about what they want to do next instead of getting started. They're waiting for an epiphany about what to do next."

And he says he tells journalists weighing a new career to think hard about that. "I want him or her to think whether he really was sick and tired of journalism," he says. "If they get into a new field, they're competing against 22-year-olds."

But when they do change fields, some find it a good thing. "Sometimes you've been wishing to do something new for a long time, and the status quo is hard to break out of," he says. "It can be a release, liberation."

In the survey I asked the former newspaper staffers if being laid off was an opportunity they'd been looking for. About 40 percent said that wasn't true at all, but for the rest, it was either absolutely true or had at least some ring of truth.

For 18 years, Joe Grimm was the recruiter for the *Detroit Free Press*. Talk about a job with a limited future these days. Grimm, 54, accepted a buyout last July and left the paper the following month. With his two boys grown, Grimm says, "I had the luxury of making less money."

Grimm says journalists must "become much better entrepreneurs."

As he has.

Grimm supports himself working as a visiting editor in residence at Michigan State University; editing at a Web site for Native Americans (reznetnews.org); editing teaching guides for the *Wall Street Journal* classroom edition; and writing the "Ask the Recruiter" column on the Poynter site (poynter.org/recruiter). He put together a collection of those columns in a self-published book.

His advice to people who still have newspaper jobs: "I would use my working hours to prepare myself" for the uncertain future that lies ahead. And, he suggests, devote nights and weekends to learning new skills—database management, say, or PhotoShop.

Like Challenger, he sees writing as one of the strengths journalists bring to their next life. But he also says they're good at "analyzing and synthesizing and making pretty quick decisions about what can and should be done." He says he knows former journalists who now work for foundations to help establish whether their money is being well spent.

But at some point, Grimm says, you have to have a pretty serious conversation with yourself. "What is it you like to do? What are you best at?" One top editor he knows "finally did something really different. He bought a franchise for an after-school golf program. He really loved golf."

Sam Amico wasn't forced out of his newspaper job at Ohio's *Sandusky Register*. He decided on his own that it was time to make a move. "In February, I turned 40, and I just didn't feel I had a future in newspapers," he says. "I saw what was going on around me, seeing friends taking buyouts or flat-out laid off."

He did what advice columns are always telling people to do: Find your passion and turn it into a job. In his case, the passion was the National Basketball Association. In 2001, while working as sports editor at Wheeling, West Virginia's *Intelligencer*, he started a weekly, electronic NBA newsletter that he e-mailed to friends and contacts in the NBA.

"I'd come home after work each Tuesday and write it, and it'd be in people's mailboxes Wednesday," he says. The newsletter caught on. People started posting it on their blogs and passing it around. By 2005, he says, "I had so much information I thought I could do a Web site and write every day." He also had enough credibility with the NBA that he has credentials to cover all its games.

About that time he divorced and moved to Sandusky to stay near his four-year-old son. He voluntarily went from full time to part time at the *Register* and then quit altogether in May 2008 to see if he could make a living off his site, probasketballnews.com.

He says advertising income from the site, which he built himself, "is very inconsistent," but he's making a living he describes as "decent." And though he loves what he's doing, like a lot of former newspaper people he misses the newsroom, the "smell of the ink and the paper. I felt more comfortable there than in my daily life."

Jay Westcott, 36, came to journalism a little later than most. He did a hitch in the Navy, then sold cars for awhile. But photography was his love. He worked his way through the Corcoran College of Art and Design by working on the picture desk at the *Washington Post* and later as a staff photographer at the *Washington Examiner*. He was "churning out" three photo assignments a day. "You're not going to get the best work that way," he says. "I felt like I was stalling in my career a bit."

On January 25, 2007, he was laid off. He went to work almost immediately for the International Medical News Group but kept getting calls for freelance work. "You need to know what you like to do, what you want to do, and own it," he says. For him that was editorial portraiture. In August 2007, he quit his job and started freelancing full time.

"Sometimes it's stressful, waiting for the checks to come in," he says, echoing the lament of freelancers everywhere. But he's getting a steady stream of assignments. He shoots an average of six days a month for *Washingtonian* magazine. In July, he had 22 shooting days altogether.

"For the most part I'm much happier," he says. "Honestly, looking back, [getting laid off] was the best thing that ever happened to me."

Joanne Cleaver, 50, spent the first 23 years of her career freelancing as a business writer in Chicago. During that time she did research for *Working Woman* magazine on the top 25 companies for women executives. But she felt she needed to work as an editor at a newspaper. In 2004, she and her family moved to Milwaukee, where she became a deputy business editor of the *Journal Sentinel*.

When she accepted a buyout, leaving the paper in August 2008, she says, "I was really well positioned. . . . I never let go of my freelancing." Her advice to others still working at papers is a variation on Grimm's: "Trade on the position and title while you have it."

While Cleaver, Grimm, Amico and Westcott are all still in journalism after leaving newspapers, Patrick O'Driscoll and Mike Peluso took another popular escape route. They went into media relations. Both are happier men for it, and not because they're making a pile of money. They were both better paid in their newspaper jobs.

O'Driscoll, 56, had the kind of career young journalists dream about. After graduating from the University of Nevada, Reno in 1975, he went to work for Gannett's Reno *Evening Gazette* and Nevada *State Journal*. In 1983, Gannett was plucking reporters from its smaller papers across the country to staff its high-profile start-up, *USA Today*. O'Driscoll was one of them. "It was a pretty good gig," he recalls. "Quite a lot of travel."

The six-month temporary assignment at *USA Today* lasted six years, but O'Driscoll missed the West and the mountains. In 1989, he became the roaming Western regional reporter for the *Denver Post*. "They gave me $500 more a year and a company car," he says.

Eight years later he was back with *USA Today*, opening the paper's Denver bureau. He covered the Columbine school shooting, the JonBenet Ramsey murder investigation, the Kobe Bryant saga, the Salt Lake City Olympics, Hurricane Katrina.

But about five years ago, O'Driscoll felt the paper's "philosophy and story focus" at the time didn't leave him the opportunity "to tell the stories I wanted to tell." On December 21, 2007, he took a buyout that included 48 weeks' pay. Days before, he had covered shootings at two Colorado churches that left five people dead.

"That was the last media herd thing I had to cover," he says, remembering the 12-degree weather as he stood outside waiting for a press conference. "All of that told me, 'Yeah, another reason I'm not going to miss this job.'"

In April 2008, four months after taking the *USA Today* buyout, he went to work as a public affairs specialist for the Intermountain Regional Headquarters of the National Park Service in Denver. "They were looking for a veteran journalist who could write and was adaptable," he says. In his new job he handles media relations and writes news releases and the employee newsletter as well as speeches.

"I thought I would have a period of mourning having left the newspaper business," he says. "I didn't." He adds, "There's something to be said for dialing it back. It's not as all-consuming as newspapering."

O'Driscoll says he has learned this overarching lesson: "Second and third acts can start in your mid-50s."

Peluso, 59, started his second or third act in 2002 when he was laid off by the online division of the *St. Paul Pioneer Press*, then owned by now-defunct Knight Ridder, where he'd worked in a variety of editing jobs since 1980, including, at one point, news editor. "That was the toughest job I ever had," he says. "Twelve hours a day without even a coffee break. Any meal I ate, I ate at my desk. It was brutal."

He got almost a year's severance pay and within a month was working as a writer and editor at the University of Minnesota Foundation, where he's now director of marketing analytics and technology. "It's a terrific place to work, and it's very stable," he says.

"I miss the newsroom that I left," Peluso adds. "I don't miss what I'm certain it became." He describes newspapers today as "continually reining in ambitions."

At newspapers today, "there's no other way to feel other than beat down, and I'm glad I'm not there to be beat down," he says. "My blood pressure is at least 20 points better than when I was in the newsroom. That's no lie," he says, adding, "Getting laid off six years ago was the best thing that ever happened to me."

"We were there at the top, the best time to be in it," he says. "The '80s were a blast, the '90s were a bit more stressful, but the last few years—who'd want to be there?"

When a Newspaper Falls in the Forest . . .*

By Robin Peek
Information Today, June 2009

I find it ironic that the medium where we read the most about the demise of the daily newspaper happens to be a newspaper. This is not to say that other media are not covering it; indeed many of the giant media companies are holding the debt on these media properties.

Of course, the passing of the daily newspaper has been predicted for decades, long before the web went mainstream. Historians will note that every new mass media once threatened the previous one, and yet somehow they adapted. The newspaper, the magazine, the radio, and the television: Each adapted and now co-exists with the others. It wasn't perfect; there were failures. But it also gave rise to success stories, even if it meant the number of traditional media outlets would fall under the likes of CNN, first in cable and then everywhere else. And then there is the eye candy of *USA Today*, the nation's newspaper.

The web demonstrated all sorts of ways to have media meltdowns. The Internet Archive's Wayback Machine is littered with the remains of web media efforts that crashed. If they would have fallen in the forest, there wouldn't have been many in the woods to hear them fall. The memory of them fades quickly, and unless you know the name of the media effort in question, it's difficult to recover them. These snapshots came and went even more quickly into that pixel cemetery known as the InternetArchive, sometimes with so little fanfare that the mention of their deaths was not covered by an "authoritative source."

NO EASY ANSWERS

Several things happened at once to cause this epidemic of newspaper demise. Of course, the economy gets the first blame (as it should), but many newspaper properties were already in financial turmoil with declining advertising revenues and papers getting thinner and thinner. Despite valiant efforts by the newspaper companies to encourage readers to read a paper while tuning into their iPods, even older readers left the flock.

At one time, the Sunday edition of *The New York Times* landed on our doorstep with such a loud thud that we could hear it anywhere in the condo. But over the years, the paper became so light that we would have to go to the door to see if it had even arrived. Eventually it ceased arriving altogether as we became yet another household that preferred to get its coverage online. For my husband, who I knew would be the late adapter to the online approach, his moment came when *The Times* dropped its coverage of a television schedule in the print edition. He found that the coverage was much better online: The layout is better, the ink didn't rub off on his hands, and if he woke up at 5:30 in the morning, the news was right there waiting for him. Even on his vintage laptop, he is a happy news reader.

Two other things happened at this interesting apex that changed the fate of the daily paper. The "green movement" was already gaining steam before economic issues remarkably made "green" a way to make more "gold." While the motivation may truly be to save the Earth with the secondary motivation to save money, being green is the new machine. Even here in Harvard country there are banners proclaiming that "Green is the New Crimson" (of course, crimson is Harvard's color). I have often wondered how many international visitors have been confused by this language. Rumors abound of tourists in pursuit of Harvard's new green logo to adorn their T-shirts.

Green is pretty mean to mainstream newspapers. Just last week in class, one of my students (whose small town does not have curbside recycling) noticed how much newsprint she was hauling to the recycling location. That caused a change in behavior, so much so that she can hardly get her dad's Kindle 2 away from him now. As for my students, if they want information about the weather, they practically have been trained from birth to go to the web to find it. Now many of them get such information from their iPhones. The thought of looking up the weather or sports scores in a newspaper seems quaint.

DEALING WITH NEW PROBLEMS

As the newsrooms grow empty, we are left with some fascinating questions. If the print edition has long been considered the publication of record by many librarians and publishers, what provisions will be needed when a newspaper goes to an online-only edition? And if a newspaper completely shutters its doors, what will the authoritative source be that replaces it? Local bloggers? Local television news sites? Will communities create some local content management system tailored to their specific needs?

Alternatively, writer-driven websites such as Helium, which declares itself to be the face of the publishing revolution, are attempting to fill the void. While I have covered news about this website in prior columns, it has matured from its earlier incarnations. Already the Helium website opens announcing "Looking for Your Local Newspaper," establishing partnerships with more than a half-dozen newspapers. The same website also announced a partnership with the Society for Professional Journalists.

The demise of many newspapers was inevitable. They stopped doing things that could be done better on the web, much like a patient who was getting ill for years. Circumstances only hastened the prognosis. But what will fill the void in a community when the unifying fabric of a newspaper is gone? Or will there simply be a void? And will the concept of news "authority" take on new meaning?

Self-Inflicted Wounds[*]

By John Morton
American Journalism Review, October/November 2006

Few things are as they used to be, so it's no surprise that newspapers are among the traditional institutions that have changed greatly over the years.

Looking back over my own close scrutiny of newspapers, which covers roughly the last half of the 20th century to the present, I am struck most of all by a decline in what I refer to as the "standing" of newspapers.

Standing encompasses many things: prevalence, respect, influence, personality, reputation and, most of all, relevance. Some of the decline was inevitable, due to the emergence of competing media such as television and the Internet and changes in the economic underpinning of the newspaper business. But some of it was self-inflicted.

One way to measure prevalence is to tally the number and circulation of newspapers. In 1950 there were 1,772 dailies with a total circulation of 53.8 million and 549 Sunday papers with 46.6 million. But since 1980, the number and circulation of dailies has declined fairly steadily, slipping to 1,452 last year, with circulation down to 53.3 million—below where it was 55 years ago, despite nearly a doubling in the size of the national population. The number of Sunday papers has increased, to 914 last year, but their circulation began to decline in the late 1990s and dropped to 55.3 million last year.

The drop in the number of dailies, especially in the early years, reflected the emergence of television as a competitor for leisure time and advertising, which helped kill off numerous afternoon papers.

While the decline in the number of dailies and the number of competitive markets has generally not helped the quality of newspaper journalism, it has had a salutary effect on the financial health of those that remain. Profitability of newspapers has improved fairly steadily over the last 30 years. In the first six months of this year, not a particularly good one for the newspaper business, the average operating profit was a robust 18 percent.

The other elements that make up standing—respect, influence and the like—are subjective and difficult to quantify, but there is no denying that numerous surveys of readers and nonreaders show lower levels of confidence in and respect for newspapers.

This is due at least in part to the growing ideological partisanship of the nation: Democrat and Republican, liberal and conservative, secular and evangelical, anti-death penalty and pro-death penalty, pro-choice and anti-abortion—the list could go on and on. These divisions have become very intense. Most newspapers try to cover contentious issues even-handedly, which, while virtuous, tends to offend both sides.

But some of the decline in standing can be blamed on newspapers themselves. While the drop in the number of newspapers was inevitable because of economic forces beyond their control, other facets of decline were self-imposed.

Mostly gone now are dailies that sought to extend their circulation and influence over a wide region, in some cases entire states. Large chains acquired many such papers and quickly eliminated circulation much beyond a paper's home market, for the simple reason that the papers spent more to print and deliver distant circulation than they made from it. Also largely scrapped were the news bureaus that supported the circulation.

Concentration of ownership has created a newspaper industry that puts high profits over quaint notions about a newspaper's obligation to be a beacon of knowledge for as wide an area as possible. The standing of these newspapers inevitably declined.

Similarly, the quest for profit has diminished many newspapers' efforts to bring their own stamp to covering events throughout the world. In recent years many newspapers have announced the closing of foreign bureaus; *Newsday* and the *Baltimore Sun* are two recent examples. True, major newspapers will parachute journalists into hot spots like Iraq, but the nuanced reporting from foreign locales that once graced many newspapers is increasingly hard to find.

Newspapers also have become smaller and less imposing as the industry has adopted narrower web widths and lighter-weight newsprint to save money. Even the *Wall Street Journal* and the *New York Times*, long holdouts, are joining the trend.

Finally, many newspapers have started to undermine their dignity by offering up parts of their section fronts, and even front pages, to advertisers. It was always comforting to pick up a newspaper and peruse a front page and section fronts unsullied by advertising—room enough for that on inside pages. Again, the quest for profit.

Many of these developments, considered individually, may not seem of great consequence. Collectively, they remind me of death by a thousand cuts. All have contributed to the decline in the standing of newspapers at a time when, more than ever, they need to stand tall.

3

Media Bias: The Politics of Journalism

Editor's Introduction

Media bias is not a new phenomenon. Throughout history people have reported events through particular prisms or from specific vantage points, allowing nationality, culture, political ideology, religious theology, and/or naked self-interest to influence their coverage. The notion of "unbiased" news coverage is a fairly recent and largely American development. By the same measure, concerns about media bias tend to be more pronounced in the United States than elsewhere. Overseas, people generally expect that news sources, whether they're protected by press freedoms or not, will have some sort of slant, official or otherwise, and aren't much bothered by it. For example, newspapers in Great Britain are widely associated with political agendas, even actual political parties. In fact, the *Daily Telegraph* is often called the *Daily Torygraph* due to its close affiliation with the British Conservative or Tory Party.

In the United States, however, media bias is a serious subject and stands at the center of an ongoing national debate. This may seem paradoxical, given the exalted place freedom of the press holds in the United States, enshrined as it is in the Bill of Rights to our Constitution. A free press, one presumes, has the right to be a biased one. Nevertheless, the debate rages on, whether one watches Fox News or MSNBC.

The most common and loudest charge is that mainstream news organizations slant their coverage in a liberal direction. The "liberal media" is a frequent rhetorical target of conservative politicians and pundits. Throughout his time in office, President Richard Nixon often took aim at what he perceived as a general lack of journalistic objectivity, and nowadays this perception has only become more widespread, with those on the right regularly lampooning the so-called liberal media and such mainstream news organizations as *The New York Times*. In supporting their case they cite "Rathergate," when CBS News failed to authenticate documents used to support a story alleging that former President George W. Bush failed to fulfill his Texas Air National Guard duty during the early 1970s. Most experts agreed the documents in question were forgeries, and the subsequent outcry led to a major shakeup at CBS and the resignation of the network's longtime anchorman Dan Rather. While some saw the incident as an example of the perils of sloppy reporting, many conservatives saw evidence of a liberal media conspiracy designed to influence the outcome of the 2004 election.

But the complaints don't all come from the political right. Liberals frequently critique the news media, too. Most often they direct their ire at cable television's Fox News Channel, declaring the network's tagline, "Fair and Balanced," an outrageous joke. They also point to media coverage of President George W. Bush's charges that Iraq under Saddam Hussein possessed weapons of mass destruction (WMDs) in the run-up to the Iraq War. Employed to justify the use of force by the United States and its allies, these charges were not borne out by subsequent findings, and many blamed the press for not investigating them with more skepticism as the president was building public support for the invasion of Iraq and the overthrow of Hussein.

The problem goes deeper than mere partisan politics, however. Many see regional and cultural fault lines influencing news coverage. Some view the mainstream media, based largely in the "Left Coast" cities of New York and Los Angeles, California, with their cosmopolitan sensibilities, as out of touch with the values of mainstream American, the so-called "heartland."

Whatever truth there may be to these charges and countercharges is hard to discern. Humans come equipped with their own individual biases and have the annoying habit of reading them into everything. Different facts and figures can be marshalled to support one argument or another. Specific incidents can be used to prove one's case. In the meantime, both sides have their talking points.

The articles collected in this chapter consider media bias, the media-bias industry, and the larger impact they are having on how news is gathered and consumed. In the first selection, "The Bias Wars," Joe Strupp offers a broad examination of the subject. Among the statistics he cites are those that indicate that, as a profession, journalism attracts more liberals into its fold than conservatives. However, whether and how this influences news coverage remains an open question.

The following selection, "In the Tank?" features analysis by Paul Farhi, who contends that charges of bias in the mainstream media are overblown. However, as technology and economics have transformed the news business, the commitment to objective reporting among journalists is showing signs of diminishing. One possible outcome, according to Farhi, is that the news will become even "more interpretive, more personal, more subjective and more opinionated." In other words, "All those complaints about bias you've been hearing lately? You haven't heard anything yet."

While acknowledging that the press has flaws, Evan Thomas contends that much of the criticism misses the mark. In the next piece, "The Myth of Objectivity," Thomas declares that mainstream journalism is "prejudiced, but not ideologically," he writes. "The press's real bias is for conflict." Scandals, riots, disasters—that's what motivates the media, not some insidious political agenda.

In "Red Media, Blue Media," two *Washington Post* reporters discuss a study they conducted to determine whether people prefer to receive their news from sources they believe have views similar to their own. The data showed a marked polarization, with Republicans and Democrats preferring "conservative" and "liberal" sources, respectively. The authors conclude that in the future, "the very same lines that divide voters will also divide news audiences."

On the political right, it is established doctrine that most major news organizations slant their coverage in a liberal direction, hence the constant criticism of the "liberal media." However, as Ted J. Smith III points out in "Public Sees Media Bias," these views aren't limited to conservatives. Indeed, a plurality of the public see the media as either very or somewhat liberal.

Due to recent changes in the media landscape, fewer journalists are out in the field, researching stories and uncovering the news. These days, more and more partisans are doing the legwork that formerly fell to news professionals and passing their findings to the press and from there to the public. One recent example of this phenomenon is explored by Mark Bowden in the final piece in this chapter, "The Story Behind the Story." When President Obama nominated Sandra Sotomayor to serve on the Supreme Court, conservatives had already done their opposition research, tracking a few suspect comments Sotomayor had made at legal forums over the years. With the clips in hand, the mainstream media then transmitted them to the public. Bowden sees this trend as troubling, emphatically stating, "The honest, disinterested voice of a true journalist carries an authority that no self-branded liberal or conservative can have."

The Bias Wars[*]

By Joe Strupp
Editor & Publisher, August 2004

Michael Rowett may be the last *Arkansas Democrat-Gazette* reporter anyone expected to leave for a job with the Democratic Party. Just four years ago, Rowett broke the story that several members of a state ethics committee investigating President Bill Clinton had given contributions to either Clinton or the Democrats. "He went after that as a thorough and dogged reporter, not knowing what he would find," recalls Griffin Smith, *Democrat-Gazette* executive editor.

"He was a stalwart of capital coverage. I had no idea what his politics were." So when Rowett gave up reporting to become communications director for the Arkansas State Democratic Party in May, Smith was as surprised as anyone. "He had strong political views, strong enough to leave journalism for a job with a political party," Smith observes. "But they didn't get reflected in his coverage."

But is this the norm in many other newsrooms? And did Rowett's political leanings really remain completely disconnected from his work? Some might even argue that he dug harder into the Clinton story because he did not want to appear soft on the party he favored.

In today's increasingly divisive political climate—and highly scrutinized media landscape—constant attention focuses on the real or potential bias of reporters and editors. As reputable polls continue to suggest that most journalists are moderate or liberal, with relatively few conservatives, questions mount: What effect do political beliefs and social values have on news coverage? Are newsrooms politically imbalanced? And if so, what could or should be done to correct that?

A recent survey by the Pew Research Center, which appeared to uphold the notion of an ideological tilt in newsrooms—both print and broadcast—only added fuel to the fire. It suggested that self-described moderates dominate the newsroom, but liberals outnumber conservatives by a ratio of about 5-to-1 at larger print outlets and about 3-to-1 at local papers. National Public Radio ombudsman

Jeffrey Dworkin commented that these findings are "likely to follow news organizations around for the rest of the political year like Marley's ghost."

Journalism veterans interviewed by *E&P* disagree about why an ideological schism exists. Some say fewer conservatives enter journalism because the profession offers modest financial rewards and promotes aggressive questioning of the establishment. As Tribune Media Services columnist Cal Thomas put it, "It's just not the kind of thing conservatives do." But others contend that conservatives feel unwelcome in today's newsrooms because they contradict the "group think," to quote one editor.

But if left-leaning journalists outnumber those on the right in newsrooms, what does that really mean for the end product? Can a reporter or editor be *truly* objective? Should they even try? What is a liberal or conservative, anyway? Do the historical definitions come even close to describing the mishmash of views many people hold?

E&P sought to probe some of these issues with a fresh eye, and with our particular audience in mind (while recognizing that follow-up reports would be required). In addition to speaking with j-school chairs and media critics, we also interviewed—at length—nearly two dozen editors at a cross-section of newspapers, from Tacoma, Wash., to Tampa, Fla. Far too much attention on this issue has focused on a handful of national papers, and even more so, on network and cable news. We wanted to look at how this debate plays out in the wider range of news outlets read by tens of millions of Americans each day.

Yet we are also aware of the outsized importance of the national outlets. Many smaller papers carry wire and news service articles beamed in from afar, and the national media sets the tone for coverage everywhere. Fran Coombs, managing editor of *The Washington Times*, warns that even papers with balanced ideological staffs often pick up *New York Times* articles or use syndicates perceived by some to be left-leaning.

Although views, of course, vary, what was most surprising in talking to editors was that, after all the controversy, so few acknowledged that a political imbalance

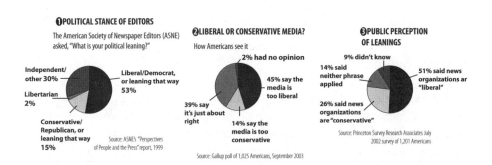

① POLITICAL STANCE OF EDITORS

The American Society of Newspaper Editors (ASNE) asked, "What is your political leaning?"

Independent/other 30%

Liberal/Democrat, or leaning that way 53%

Libertarian 2%

Conservative/Republican, or leaning that way 15%

Source: ASNE's "Perspectives of People and the Press" report, 1999

② LIBERAL OR CONSERVATIVE MEDIA?

How Americans see it

2% had no opinion

45% say the media is too liberal

39% say it's just about right

14% say the media is too conservative

Source: Gallup poll of 1,025 Americans, September 2003

③ PUBLIC PERCEPTION OF LEANINGS

9% didn't know

14% said neither phrase applied

51% said news organizations ar "liberal"

26% said news organizations are "conservative"

Source: Princeton Survey Research Associates July 2002 survey of 1,201 Americans

exists at their paper or, if it does, that it was anything they were particularly concerned about or acting vigorously to correct. The majority of editors said they did not care about the ideological makeup of their staffs, and they seemed to sincerely believe that professionalism—their own, and their reporters'—regularly overcomes any personal beliefs.

None of the editors said they had ever asked potential reporters about their political leanings, or plan to in the future, and few believe an "ideological affirmative action program" is needed to bring more conservatives into newsrooms.

WHAT THE NUMBERS SHOW

While it may seem like a recent phenomenon, the debate over alleged liberal bias in newsrooms has simmered for decades now, going back to the Nixon era when Vice President Spiro Agnew attacked the "nattering nabobs of negativity" in the press.

Evidence from polling was slow to surface until a 1981 survey of 240 journalists at national news outlets by S. Robert Lichter and Stanley Rothman found that 81% of that "media elite" sample said they voted for Democratic candidates for president in every election between 1964 and 1976. Lichter, now president of the Center for Media and Public Affairs (CMPA), a Washington, D.C.-based research organization, jokes that he became "the flavor of the month for conservatives" when that study was released.

Since then, a wide variety of surveys have probed deeper, though results have generally agreed that the national press skews further to the left than the general public (the local press, somewhat less so).

A 1985 *Los Angeles Times* study of 2,700 journalists at 621 newspapers found this sample to the left of the public on issues relating to abortion, gun control, prayer in schools and defense spending.

Like Lichter's 1981 study, some surveys focused strictly on the elite but were then wrongly cited by others to suggest all reporters reflect that pattern. In 1999,

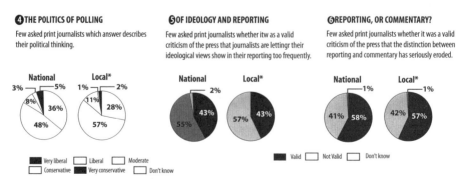

❹ THE POLITICS OF POLLING

Few asked print journalists which answer describes their political thinking.

❺ OF IDEOLOGY AND REPORTING

Few asked print journalists whether it was a valid criticism of the press that journalists are letting their ideological views show in their reporting too frequently.

❻ REPORTING, OR COMMENTARY?

Few asked print journalists whether it was a valid criticism of the press that the distinction between reporting and commentary has seriously eroded.

National: 3% — 5%, 8%, 36%, 48%
Local*: 1% — 2%, 11%, 28%, 57%

■ Very liberal □ Liberal □ Moderate
□ Conservative ■ Very conservative □ Don't know

National: 2%, 43%, 55%
Local*: 57%, 43%

National: 1%, 41%, 58%
Local*: 1%, 42%, 57%

■ Valid □ Not Valid □ Don't know

*The "local" category includes newspapers from a list of the top 100 newspapers ranked by circ, excluding 16 newspapers selected for the national sample.

Charts 4, 5, and 6 source: The Pew Research Center

the American Society of Newspaper Editors kept a narrow focus, surveying 1,037 reporters at 61 newspapers of all sizes. It found that 53% said they were liberal or Democrat or leaned that way, and only 15% called themselves Republican or conservative or tilted that way. The trend was not as evident at smaller papers, but still existed.

All of these surveys covered mainly reporters. But what about editors? In January 1998, a survey commissioned by *E&P* of 167 editors around the country found much less of an imbalance, with 57% saying they voted for Clinton in 1996, versus 49% of the public. Only 14% said that journalists "often" let their opinions influence their coverage, with 57% conceding this "sometimes" happened.

As poll results emerged and partisan groups and news outlets fanned the flames, public perception of bias—or at least a growing tendency to complain about it—grew. It culminated, many argue, in the creation of Fox News, and inspired books such as Bernard Goldberg's 2001 bestseller *Bias*. An Indiana University School of Journalism survey in 2002 found that Democrats topped Republicans by about a 2-1 margin in news rooms, but the number of Democrats (37%) was at its lowest ebb since 1971.

And what of the public view of all this? In September 2003, a Gallup Poll found that 60% of self-described conservatives think the news media is too liberal, as did 40% of moderates and even 18% of liberals. A growing number of liberals, about 30%, feel the media slants to the right, a view promoted by Eric Alterman in his book, *What Liberal Media?*

The bias war was now raging. In this setting, the Pew report on newsroom attitudes released this year on May 23 was certain to set off sparks (see results below). The following month, another Pew survey of the general public found that conservatives now distrust just about every major media outlet. Even *The Wall Street Journal*'s "believability" quotient among Republicans has plunged, without apparent cause.

Does that mean that most media outlets are biased, and increasingly so, or just that more people today, left and right, are looking for news coverage that validates, rather than tests, their world view—and when it doesn't, they charge "bias"? Bruce Bartlett, a senior fellow at the National Center for Policy Analysis, doesn't quite see it that way, believing that bias "jumps out at readers from time to time, and rather than write or call to complain, they say, 'I'm tired of reading that liberal claptrap,' and just cancel their subscriptions."

In any case, if there are more liberals than conservatives in newsrooms, why is that? Editors disagree, but many point to the traditional mission of the news business, particularly newspapers, to be a public watchdog and challenger of authority. Also, there always seems to be a steady stream of advocacy-oriented journalism school graduates ready to re-stock newsrooms.

'TYPICAL' NEWSROOMS

Journalism professors across the country are noticing skyrocketing numbers of students choosing to study public relations. It is the fastest-growing major over the last decade at Syracuse University. A lot of students at Syracuse, in fact, start out majoring in newspaper or broadcast and decide to switch to public relations. Lee Coppola, chair of the journalism department at St. Bonaventure University in Olean, N.Y., says 75%-80% of his students have no interest in being daily reporters.

A commonly held belief is that one's political persuasion factors into the eventual career choice, that a liberal student is more inclined to take a job at a newspaper, while a conservative is more likely to choose public relations, advertising or broadcasting. There's anecdotal evidence for this, but no polling data. However, it would explain why the liberal tilt in newsrooms seems to endure as years pass.

Bob Zelnick, chair of the journalism department at Boston University, disagrees. "If a journalism school graduate goes into public relations, it's more because of the economy," he says. "They may have found a journalism job unsatisfying or they are in debt and need a higher-paying career."

A more unusual theory comes from Professor David Baron of Stanford University, who in a February 2004 research paper theorized that profit-hungry news corporations tolerate leftward bias because it helps them attract liberal journalists who tend to accept working for a lower wage. Thus liberal bias "is shown to be consistent with profit maximization."

Indeed, observes executive editor Smith of the *Democrat-Gazette*, "There are probably more social reformers in journalism than accountants. We tend to attract a certain kind of person."

But by the same token, do newsrooms tend to deflect certain kinds of people? Smith admits conservatives may not feel as wanted in newsrooms if they believe they are dominated by liberals and moderates: "Conservatives need to feel welcomed."

Cal Thomas, known to take a conservative viewpoint now and then, backs the "unwelcome" argument, but adds that the profession "doesn't pay all that well unless you get to a certain level," discouraging many conservatives. Larry King, executive editor of the Omaha (Neb.) *World-Herald*, agrees that conservatives "have more of a background that is perhaps more attuned to the financial aspects of the world."

William McGowan, media critic and author of *Coloring the News: How Political Correctness Has Corrupted American Journalism*, disagrees, arguing that plenty of conservatives seek to enter journalism, and not only feel unwelcome but are barred from jobs because of their beliefs. "It is mainly a self-selecting group," says McGowan. "They get stopped at the door."

Joe Worley, executive editor of the *Tulsa* (Okla.) *World*, confirms that more conservatives are interested in news than in the past, but not necessarily newspapers:

❼ WHERE GRADS SEEK WORK

Types of jobs sought by journalism & mass
communication bachelor degree recipients (in 2002)

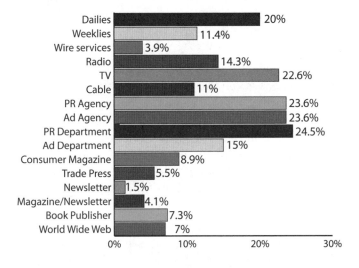

Dailies	20%
Weeklies	11.4%
Wire services	3.9%
Radio	14.3%
TV	22.6%
Cable	11%
PR Agency	23.6%
Ad Agency	23.6%
PR Department	24.5%
Ad Department	15%
Consumer Magazine	8.9%
Trade Press	5.5%
Newsletter	1.5%
Magazine/Newsletter	4.1%
Book Publisher	7.3%
World Wide Web	7%

Percentages do not add up to 100% because graduates apply to more than one type of job.

Source: Annual Survey of Journalism & Mass Communication Graduates, Grady College
of Journalism & Mass Communication, University of Georgia; U.S. Bureau of Labor Statistics

"There are a lot more conservative journalists out there, but they are often attracted to publications that espouse their conservative view."

NO AFFIRMATIVE ACTION?

Despite the imbalance, few editors interviewed by *E&P* consider recruiting conservatives a priority in today's era of budget cutbacks and revenue problems. In fact, only a handful would even guess at the ideological makeup of their newsroom, and fewer still ask about a potential reporter's political views in a job interview.

"I don't know the politics of my newsroom, and I don't care to hear them," declares Rich Oppel, editor of the *Austin* (Texas) *American-Statesman* and the father of two reporters. "I am interested in their professional skills, and their professionalism. For me, your politics are not important." When asked if he would question a job applicant about his or her political leanings, Oppel offers a resounding "No," but adds, "I will ask questions that allow them to meander into that area; where they grew up, what the talk was at the dinner table, how much they read."

William "Skip" Hidlay, executive editor of the *Asbury Park Press* in Neptune, N.J., also dismisses much of the ideological chatter, citing strong journalistic skills as the key for reporters. "I have never asked a reporting or editing candidate their political beliefs. I don't think it's valuable," he says. "In my opinion, it is irrelevant because good people keep political leanings out of their stories."

Dennis Ryerson, editor of *The Indianapolis Star*, says it's different, however, when it comes to hiring political activists, explaining why his paper had turned away an applicant for an editorial page position "who had recent involvement in an anti-abortion group."

Jim Witt, executive editor of the *Fort Worth* (Texas) *Star-Telegram*, warns against sacrificing the best possible newsroom talent available to achieve political diversity. Says Witt, "you can't put together a newspaper like a football team."

Most editors, in fact, punted when asked to define "liberal," "moderate" or "conservative." This is a confusing era, after all, when it's the Democrats who rail against budget deficits and the Republicans who champion foreign intervention. "The label stuff bores me," says Charlie Waters, executive editor of *The Fresno* (Calif.) *Bee*, who also pooh-poohed efforts to dig into employee ideologies. "To me, it's a non-starter."

Such attitudes may be surprising at a time when newspapers are desperately seeking more diversity in the hiring of women, blacks and other minorities, a mission that strongly surfaces at annual journalism conferences hosted by the American Society of Newspaper Editors (ASNE) and the Associated Press Managing Editors (APME). Media critic McGowan portrays it this way: "You put so many diversity czars in charge, and their priority is to recruit journalists of color." If the urgency of getting other minorities into newsrooms is so great, why isn't it equally important to have an ideological balance?

"I don't think it is the same thing," replies Ryerson. "I can see why we look at the number of women, the number of blacks or other minorities. I don't think it is fair to assess the political leanings of a newsroom."

Cal Thomas recalls a visit to a Texas newspaper years ago, which he declined to identify, where he says he saw an ad for a gay reporter on the wall. But he doesn't want to see ads for conservatives either. "I don't think you ought to be advertising for that: Democrat, Republican, gay, straight, Catholic, or Jew," Thomas says. "It hurts the industry. It's like cafeteria journalism." Like some others, he may believe that the last thing the industry needs is more reporters with an ideological chip on their shoulder.

John Leo, columnist for *U.S. News & World Report* and frequent critic of the liberal newsroom, tells *E&P*, "The last thing anybody would want is a conservative quota. But I think editors should try to have diversity in editorial conferences—people of all backgrounds, religions and opinions. We all know that conferences changed the day the first black attended. And it was a very good thing. . . . I don't care how many Democrats or liberals there are in the newsroom, so long as we do something to change the one-note newsroom culture."

But a handful of newsroom veterans and others do argue for making an extra effort to hire more conservatives. "I wish we had more conservatives in the newsroom to give us a more balanced report," admits David Zeeck, executive editor of *The News Tribune* in Tacoma, Wash., which he claims has a "fairly liberal" news staff. "I think the liberalism can show up in a kind of 'group think' here."

Editorial Director Ken Chandler of the *Boston Herald* concurs. "I'm all for diversity in every respect," he says. "Racial diversity and political diversity."

When asked how to get more conservative reporters and editors into the business, observers suggest ideas ranging from broader recruitment at colleges not traditionally known for journalists, to giving those in other professions a shot at the daily miracle.

"Don't always go to liberal arts colleges to recruit; you can go to business colleges," says Ben Marrison, editor of *The Columbus* (Ohio) *Dispatch*. Tom Rosenstiel, former dean of the Columbia University Graduate School of Journalism and director of the Project for Excellence in Journalism, agrees. "We can also look for career switchers," adds Rosenstiel, whose group co-sponsored the May 2004 Pew survey. "People with varied kinds of backgrounds, ex-teachers, ex-military and whatever to broaden the perspective." Even so, are there enough conservatives out there with a true interest in journalism to make much of an ideological inroad?

CAN PROS WRITE STRAIGHT PROSE?

Now, hold on. Even if there are more centrists and left-leaners at today's newspapers, does that really affect day-to-day reporting?

Some inside newsrooms seem to think so. In the recent Pew survey of newsroom attitudes, about four in 10 of their sample declared that journalists too often let their ideological views show in their reporting. But most editors interviewed by *E&P* contend that good reporting trumps any ideological background.

"Most of us have a level of professionalism that filters that out," says Doug Clifton, editor of *The Plain Dealer* in Cleveland. "Does that mean our biases don't creep in? No. But you emphasize a professional obligation and ensure the editing is rigorous." Karin Winner, editor of *The San Diego Union-Tribune*, agrees. "I think we know how to turn off our affiliation when we walk through the door," she says. "It does not come up."

How does this play in Peoria? Says Jack Brimeyer, managing editor of the Peoria, Ill., *Journal Star*: "We always talk about different ways of doing things and we don't have an agenda." But he adds: "Maybe it is so subtle that those of us inside the newspaper don't see it."

Some point to less obvious influences that reporters' and editors political leanings can have, including choice of stories, decisions on news placement, and even how much space to give a source.

"There are subtleties that you have to look at," comments Thomas Mitchell, editor of the *Las Vegas Review-Journal*, who took the issue head-on in a recent column that surveyed his newsroom and found, in this conservative area, that more than half were moderate, 28% liberal, and 15% conservative. "It helps to have a few people recognizing that there are two points of view on things."

Frank Denton, editor and vice president of *The Tampa* (Fla.) *Tribune*, agrees. "What we do is very subjective, and it has to be challenged by checks and balances," he says, citing reader reaction to his paper's coverage of the ongoing violence in Iraq. "Some readers have said we are not reporting enough of the good news. That was a reminder to make sure we talk about the rebuilding that is going on, as well."

VALUES COUNT, TOO

But not everything, or perhaps, anything, can be simply viewed through a "left" or "right" lens, or political-party affiliation. Values, culture, religious interest, even sports and hobbies can factor in.

"We live lives different from our readers," admits editor Ryerson of the *Indianapolis Star*. "We typically have higher educations, higher incomes, and many of us don't do the things our readers do."

Mike Connor, executive editor of *The Post-Standard* in Syracuse, N.Y., believes "the greater bias is often a narrative bias—that there is or is not a story here. I don't think it is political; it is more [about] lifestyle and social issues." Connor notes the sometimes one-sided coverage of gun rights, saying, "we don't do enough stories about the pleasures of gun ownership. That it is a source of pleasure for some people." He also cites his paper's failure to cover NASCAR adequately when it first grew in popularity. "We came sort of late to it," he says. "We didn't pay too much attention to it partly because no one in the newsroom was interested in it."

Lichter, of the Center for Media and Public Affairs, says, "The backgrounds and attitudes of journalists affect the way they see the world and present the world. But that does not mean they are getting up in the morning, looking into the mirror, and saying, 'how can I screw the Republicans today?'"

A particularly significant fault line lies in the area of organized religion. Most Americans still attend religious services fairly often; most journalists, surveys suggest, only rarely. Frank Newport, editor in chief of The Gallup Poll, tells *E&P*, referring to journalists, "They don't go to church." Andrew Kohut, director of the Pew Research Center, notes that one of the big surprises of his recent poll was that journalists are much more secular than the public at large. "Religion is difficult for reporters to cover," he adds, "because they don't come from that world. That's the *real* values gap."

Indeed, one of Pew's sharpest findings this year was that while 58% of the general public holds that one must believe in God to be a truly "moral" person, only 6% of national journalists feel that way, and 18% among the local press.

CHECKS & BALANCES

Sometimes, newsroom leaders say, reacting to readers' letters and e-mails and talking to groups is enough to help keep coverage in balance. "We have readers come into our news meetings twice a week; that gives us some real input," says Bobbie Jo Buel, executive editor of the *Arizona Daily Star* in Tucson, citing a growing trend across the country. She explains, for example, that the paper's coverage of illegal immigrants crossing at the Mexican border was evened out once staffers began regular communications with American Border Patrol, a conservative group seeking to tighten control of illegal crossings. "That's a point of view of the people who live near the border that we are more likely to check in with than we had a few years ago," she says. "They raise the issue."

Nancy Conway, editor of *The Salt Lake Tribune* in Utah, offers similar experiences in her paper's coverage of a local nuclear waste dump, which has strong advocates on both sides.

Los Angeles Times Editor John Carroll noted the dangers of letting bias get in the way in a now-famous staff memo he sent out in May 2003 that warned reporters about reporting on abortion. "I want everyone to know about how serious I am about purging all political bias from our coverage," the memo said. "We may happen to live in a political atmosphere that is suffused with liberal values (and is unreflective of the nation as a whole), but we are not going to push a liberal agenda in the news pages of the *Times.*"

The memo came in reaction to a story that had just run on a Texas bill requiring abortion doctors to counsel patients that an abortion might increase their risk of breast cancer. Carroll criticized the article for failing to quote any scientific sources up front and for giving more space to the critics of the theory. "It is not until the last three paragraphs of the story that we finally surface a professor of biology and endocrinology who believes the abortion/cancer connection is valid," the memo added. "But do we quote him as to why he believes this? No. We quote his political views." Carroll now declines to discuss the issue further.

Phil Bronstein, editor of the *San Francisco Chronicle*, says some stories that are incomplete are often the victim of poor reporting, not bias. "They more often reflect a lack of knowledge," he says, but adds that his area does have a strong liberal population that can sway coverage. "There is a liberal-to-progressive political assumption in this area, and it is incumbent upon our reporters to challenge that assumption."

Bronstein cites coverage of the homeless problem in San Francisco, which can be looked at too often simply from a liberal viewpoint. "You have to keep in mind that it is not just sad times for some people," he remarks. "You've got to make sure you reflect also what the merchant thinks about the people on the sidewalk in front of his store."

Leonard Downie Jr. of *The Washington Post* has gone so far as refusing to vote since he became the *Post*'s managing editor 20 years ago, and urges his staff to follow. "Ideally, I would like everyone on the staff to be that way, but obviously I can't make them," says Downie, who has been executive editor since 1991. "I would like my mind and others to be as open as possible. All other political activism is banned. This puts us even more above the fray."

Still, there are those who say the best check and balance on perceived bias—liberal or conservative—is to simply include voices of both sides in the daily newsroom discussions. "We have a couple of conservatives in the newsroom, and occasionally in a news meeting when the group presumes a liberal approach, one of them will say, 'Hey, have we looked at it this way?'," says David Zeeck of Tacoma. "Everyone will sort of react to it—they have to."

The Columbus Dispatch's Marrison says his newsroom has similar discussions, with a fair amount of changes resulting. "We have a good mix of liberals and conservatives, based on the debates we have in the newsroom," he says. Marrison points to a recent seven-day series the paper ran on hunger, which looked at nearby food lines and soup kitchens. "One editor thought it was too biased and had too little reporting from conservative views," he explains. "We went back and re-edited it, and it turned out the one part that sparked questions had mostly liberal sources. We made some changes to make sure it was balanced."

Oppel recalls a situation during his time as editor of *The Charlotte* (N.C.) *Observer* when the paper was covering the PTL scandal (a story which resulted in a Pulitzer Prize). An evangelical graphic artist on staff helped give perspective on the religious community, including leads to sources.

In Omaha, Neb., executive editor King mentions a recent incident in which the paper changed its map of the Middle East after a business reporter who was of Palestinian descent pointed out that the wire service file did not offer clear boundaries for the West Bank and Gaza Strip. "We would not have changed it otherwise," King says. "It is a little thing, but it is something."

Still, not every editor believes a wide-ranging ideological newsroom is a requirement for such fairness debates. "I've never worked in a newsroom where someone's bias affected their work," says Charlie Waters, executive editor of *The Fresno Bee*. "Are there instances where peoples' experiences or life lead them to do certain stories? Certainly. But it is one of the roles of the editor to filter through that."

Witt of the *Star-Telegram* in Texas agrees. "That is what editing is all about," he says, adding that he has never thought about his newsroom's ideological makeup. "Before a story gets in the paper, four or five people have read it and hopefully that makes sure that no one person can decide how we're going to write a story."

OBJECTIVITY POSSIBLE?

Nearly every editor interviewed agreed that truly objective reporters don't exist, but stressed that fair reporting is still possible, and expected.

"There is no such thing as an objective human being," declares Executive Editor Peter Bhatia of *The Oregonian* in Portland. "There is such a thing as fair and truthful reporting. I think most reporters are committed to being fair." Adds Buel of the

Arizona Daily Star, "Not a single one of us is objective. But you can be curious and include the other point of view." A few editors, such Marrison in Columbus, do admit to seeking objectivity in their reporters.

"Good reporters write balanced, rounded stories," says David Cay Johnston, a Pulitzer Prize winner now covering tax issues for *The New York Times,* who has lectured widely on journalism issues. "I have worked at five major newspapers and sat next to people who held political views that ranged from fascist to communist, and I would be hard pressed to find any sign of that in their work as reporters or editors. A better test than the liberal-vs.-conservative paradigm would be ideological-vs.-non-ideological, and rounded-vs.-not rounded.

"Fundamentally, I think this is sort of a phony issue," he continues. "It's the wrong rabbit hole to go down. You want a newsroom with a wide range of voices, but I don't think that is an issue of being liberal or conservative. Very few reporters in my experience are ideological. Journalists, especially young ones, routinely discover things that show them that the world is not as they believed it to be."

Still, Robert Lichter warns of what he calls the "Socrates Syndrome," whereby "nobody knows what's best for Americans except journalists."

Several top journalism educators agree that pure objectivity is an ideal, but not a reality. Nicholas Lemann, dean of the Columbia University Graduate School of Journalism, prefers a different term altogether. Objective, he says, "implies journalism is a scientific or numerical discipline, and it's not. I am more comfortable with the term 'intellectually honest.'"

But can newspapers go too far in their effort to guard against bias or "unbalanced" stories? Where does the line get drawn between solid watchdog journalism and unfair advocacy? If newsrooms get too caught up in appearing unbiased, and perfectly "balance" every story, do they risk losing their role in reflecting community concerns or exposing wrongs?

"There is that danger," says Clifton. "You wind up being bland, and abdicating the responsibility of being a watchdog. You are better for asking the dirty questions." Says King of the *World-Herald* in Omaha, "When you choose a topic because you perceive it as an issue, that is a subjective decision. I wouldn't call it advocacy, just aggressive, investigative journalism."

Worley, the Tulsa editor, promotes grabbing an issue "if it continues to fester in the community." Austin's Oppel also doesn't believe in "advocacy journalism," but adds, "If we can improve things by marshalling information others don't have, I think we are doing our job."

BREAKING OUT OF THE MOLD

Where does this leave us (besides promising to return to this issue in the near future)? "What we are looking for is breaking out of the mold where we deny that personal experience and beliefs impact the newsroom," observes Tom Rosenstiel of the Project for Excellence in Journalism. But, as he points out, "there is no magic formula" for what comes after that.

In the end, most editors, and many others in the field, believe that the answer to charges of bias, right or left—right or wrong—is to fully embrace the basic fundamentals of accurate, fair and complete reporting, and make sure this remains the focus of newspapers. Otherwise, newspapers will continue to fall victim to the dangerous trend that finds consumers of news only reading, or listening to, what they agree with—"information segregation," as it is known.

But no one should expect the charges of "liberal bias" at newspapers to go away anytime soon—with the presidential election in full swing, hostilities continuing in Iraq, and the nation's population more politically divided than ever.

In the Tank?[*]

By Paul Farhi
American Journalism Review, June/July 2008

Allegations of media bias have been a sideshow, and sometimes the main event, of every presidential campaign of recent vintage. Critics shrieked that a line had been crossed in 1987 when the *Miami Herald* revealed Democratic frontrunner Gary Hart's relationship with Donna Rice. Five years later, George H. W. Bush complained that reporters exaggerated the extent of the recession during his term. Al Gore's aides thought the media gave him a hard time, and his opponent George W. Bush an easy ride, in 2000. And Howard Dean and John Kerry grumbled about cable TV's obsession with Dean's "scream" and Kerry's Swift Boat opponents in 2004.

Campaign '08 has offered more, often much more, of the same. Long before the last primary vote had been cast, charges of media favoritism were flying around like confetti. An incomplete list: the press savaged Hillary Clinton's campaign while going easy on her main rival, Barack Obama (a theme echoed in two memorable "Saturday Night Live" skits); worshipful reporters gave John McCain a pass during his campaign for the Republican nomination (a new book by the liberal group Media Matters for America is titled "Free Ride: John McCain and the Media"); Obama was unfairly maligned in the primaries' latter stages.

But each claim about "the media" isn't really clear-cut. Were they too tough on Hillary? Maybe at times. But didn't Clinton's campaign benefit enormously from its early press clippings, too? Her coverage during much of 2007 made her nomination sound inevitable, which helped her attract contributions, endorsements and key advisers. Didn't she also lose 11 straight primaries to Obama, a track record that would have made another candidate a media laughingstock?

In love with Obama? Maybe, but only if you don't count relatively early stories about his past drug use (*New York Times*), reports about false rumors of his "secret" Muslim upbringing (*Washington Post*) and unflattering stories about his association with a shadowy Chicago fundraiser named Tony Rezko (*Chicago Tribune*). All of these appeared before the cable-fed eruption over Obama's ties to the Rev. Jeremiah Wright, his "bitter" comments before the Pennsylvania primary and the flap about his brief association with '60s radicals William Ayers and Bernardine Dohrn.

Too easy on McCain? Surely in some instances, but the claim ignores several major caveats, such as the widespread reporting on the disarray and near-bankruptcy of his campaign last summer, when his candidacy was virtually declared dead; the stories about his gaffes (confusing Sunni and Shiite factions in Iraq, for example); and the fact that McCain's long presence on the national scene has made him one of the best-known and most-covered figures in politics. It also fails to recognize the effect of timing on campaign coverage. McCain clinched his party's nomination in early March, which shifted the media spotlight from the GOP race to the Democratic battle. In other words, there's still time. As *Newsweek*'s Evan Thomas wrote in early March, "Right now, Obama and John McCain are popular with reporters. But if the usual laws of press physics apply, the media will turn on both men before Election Day."

Nevertheless, cries of bias grow louder with each election cycle. Polls have shown rising public skepticism about the news media for decades. According to research cited by media scholar S. Robert Lichter, two-thirds of the public agreed that the press was "fair" in a survey in 1937. By 1984, only 38 percent said newspapers were "usually fair" and only 29 percent said this of television reporting. We're fast approaching zero credibility. In a national survey conducted by Sacred Heart University in Fairfield, Connecticut, in January, only 19.6 percent of respondents said they believed "all or most" reporting. An even larger portion, 23.9 percent, said they believed "little" or none of it.

What's going on here? Are we really so biased, so incapable of checking our prejudices that even the most straightforward reporting deservedly engenders suspicion? Is all of the work of the news media deserving of skepticism?

At the risk of sounding biased, no.

Leaving aside the obvious—that reporters are flawed humans who sometimes do launder their prejudices and passions in print or on the air—there are good reasons to be skeptical. The widespread perception of media unfairness doesn't necessarily confirm the existence of it. Consider the case against claims of bias:

THE MEDIA AREN'T A MONOLITH

Critics often blame "the media," as if the sins of some are the sins of all. It's not just a bland, inexact generalization; it's a slur.

The media are, of course, made up of numerous parts, many of which bear little relation to each other. "Entertainment Tonight" is the media, as is the *Christian Science Monitor* and the BBC. Reporters, columnists, copy editors, editorial writers, photographers, assignment editors, bloggers, anchors, TV pundits are all part of the media. So are magazines, newspapers, TV networks, radio stations and Web sites. Do all, or even the majority, of "the media" act in concert? Can it all be biased simultaneously? Hardly. Critics need to define their terms. Holding "the media" responsible for some perceived slight is like blaming an entire ethnic or racial group for the actions of a few of its members.

A starting point: "I think, first of all, we need to distinguish between actual journalism [news reports in print and broadcast] and the things uttered by TV personalities," says Susan Milligan, a national political reporter for the *Boston Globe*. "The latter become obsessed—based on I don't know what—with provocative topics that may or may not be all that relevant to voters. The Geraldine Ferraro comments [criticizing Obama's candidacy] and the Obama pastor story come to mind. I mean, they're both legitimate stories, but it's a bit ridiculous how so many TV shows did nonstop coverage on them, like it was 9/11 or something."

It's true, certainly, that journalists themselves have contributed to this confusion. In an ever more complicated and economically challenged media environment, the lines between reporter and pundit have gradually disappeared. Print reporters now go on TV to opine, or write blogs containing "analysis" that is thinly disguised opinion. Lichter, president of George Mason University's Center for Media and Public Affairs, believes that some of the public's antipathy toward the press has been fueled over the past few decades by the rise of the "celebrity journalist," the reporter who covers the story, then gets on television to tell viewers what to think about it.

"I think there's a feeling that journalists have overstepped their boundaries," he says. "People don't look on [journalists] the way journalists like to view themselves—as the public's tribune, speaking truth to power, standing up for the little guy. They don't look like the little guy anymore. They're part of the celebrity culture." Increasingly, he says, "people like the news but hate the news media."

Even so:

THE MEDIA AREN'T NECESSARILY MORE BIASED; IT'S JUST THAT THE MEDIA-BIAS INDUSTRY KEEPS SAYING THEY ARE.

It's not only Rush Limbaugh, with his weekly audience of millions, who inveighs against the news media's perceived unfairness. In the two decades since Limbaugh rose to prominence, an entire industry has sprung up, on the left and right, to reinforce and amplify his gospel that the dread mainstream media distort, twist and lie.

The lesser Limbaughs of talk radio have been joined by legions of bloggers whose raison d'être is to catch mainstream journalists in mistakes or misfeasance. Organized media-monitoring groups (Fairness & Accuracy In Reporting, Accuracy in Media, Media Matters for America, etc.) troll the airwaves and scour the printed page, ready to scold. Bestseller lists are studded with attacks on the press (a copy of Bernard Goldberg's media-crit tome, "Bias," has even been enshrined in the new Newseum in Washington, D.C.).

TV shows and movies are in the same game, though typically with a comedic or satiric edge. "The Colbert Report" and "The Daily Show" have raised the skewering of the media's foibles—particularly those of TV pundits—to a fine art (a "Daily Show" sketch in late February featured "correspondent" Samantha Bee reporting from the press' "Anti-Hillary War Room," located at the "Paula Jones Conference Center"). Some pundits have even credited "Saturday Night Live"'s parody of the pro-Obama press with toughening the real press' scrutiny of the candidate.

Some criticism is warranted and healthy. But there may be a darker side to all the yammering about, and hammering of, the press. "Among the greatest of the agendas [of the media-bias industry] is to destroy the credibility of the main-stream press," wrote Roy Peter Clark, the Poynter Institute vice president and senior scholar, on Poynter's Web site (poynter.org) in January. "A case can be made that sensitivity to such criticism—along with accusations that journalists are disloyal to American interests—softened the skeptical edge of the news media during the lead-up to the Iraqi war."

THE PUBLIC DOESN'T REALLY UNDERSTAND HOW THE NEWS IS MADE

That might sound elitist, except that much of the daily suspicion cast on reporters' work seems to stem from naïveté and reflexive public cynicism. Ask journalists about a recent accusation of bias and watch their eyes begin to roll. Julie Mason, the *Houston Chronicle*'s White House reporter, remembers one reader who took her to task for being "obsessed" with John Kerry during the 2004 campaign. Obsessed? She was covering his campaign. "It was my job to be with him every day," she laughs.

Another reader spotted bias in the placement of quotes in one of Mason's stories. "I'm biased," she says, "because I put the quote in after the jump, which to them means I'm trying to bury it. They don't believe you when you say you don't control where a story jumped."

A recent letter writer to the *Atlanta Journal-Constitution*'s public editor, Angela Tuck, asked: "If the AJC is against bias, why does it seem that it disproportionately endorses Democrats running for office? What is the percentage of Republican to Democrat presidential candidate endorsements? Why make endorsements anyway, as it seems to indicate which political party the staff leans toward?" Tuck patiently explained the separation between the paper's editorial board and its news staff, how the latter is obligated to deliver balanced coverage while the former renders opinions and conclusions. Still, wrote Tuck, "many readers don't believe us when we say that editorial writers don't influence the news."

THE MORE THEY KNOW, THE LESS THEY LIKE.

Some of the public's hostility is informed by, well, more information. With a few clicks of a computer mouse, viewers and readers can cross-check and double-check what reporters say—something almost impossible just a dozen or so years ago. They can also see it for themselves, live and unaltered, thanks to live cable news coverage and Internet streaming.

"We used to be people's eyes and ears at events. Now people can watch for themselves and take away their own conclusions," says Dan Balz, a veteran Washington Post political reporter. "Reporters may emphasize different things. That's not necessarily bias, it's just a different perspective."

But seeing is believing, says Jerry C. Lindsley, director of the Sacred Heart poll. "It's not like the old days when there were three sources of [TV] news," he says. "When people see a discrepancy, that leads to frustration. When a reporter leaves something out of a story and others don't, [readers] wonder why. When they use one source but not another, people may think they're not getting the whole picture."

Adds Lindsley, "People know bias when they see it."

EXCEPT THAT THEY SOMETIMES SEE IT EVEN WHEN THEY HAVEN'T.

As the Sacred Heart survey makes clear, people implicitly overstate how much news they really consume. The poll found, for example, that Americans described the *New York Times* and National Public Radio as "mostly or somewhat liberal" roughly four times more often than they described those two outlets as "mostly or somewhat conservative." Leave aside the blunt generality inherent in this. (Is all of NPR—from "Morning Edition" to "Car Talk"—"mostly or somewhat liberal?") The more important (and unasked) question about this finding is its shaky foundation. Given that only small fractions of the populace read the *Times* or listen to NPR on a regular basis, how is it that so many Americans seem to know so much about the political leanings of the *Times* and NPR?

Similarly, people ranked "PBS News" among the lowest national TV news organizations, with just 3 percent citing it as "most trusted." This might reflect the notion that trust is a function of ratings, rather than actual reporting expertise, since all of the networks that ranked above PBS in the survey had bigger audiences. But it may also say something about the sophistication of the survey's respondents. There is, after all, no such thing as "PBS News."

THE VIEW LOOKS DIFFERENT FROM INSIDE YOUR OWN MEDIA BUBBLE.

Unlike 75 years ago, when the public deemed the press more "fair," unlike even 20 years ago, readers and viewers can now live in a media world of their own choosing. A typical news consumer can now surround himself with news that fits his preconceived political sentiments. First talk radio, then cable TV and now the Internet make it possible to tailor a self-fulfilling news menu.

Is it any wonder that the world outside this bubble often looks strange and biased to those inside it?

"We now live in a period when there is no one media anymore," says Balz. "Consumers now tend to seek out the news that conforms with their view of the world. When they see something that doesn't conform, that's bias to them."

Julie Mason says "partisans" tend to have the strongest perceptions of bias, and they aren't shy about expressing them. "They're exactly like sports fans to me," she says. "As the season progresses, they get more and more myopic about their 'team.'"

SHOCKING BUT TRUE: WE'RE NOT NEARLY AS BAD AS THEY THINK.

Content analysis is a tricky thing—a lot depends on how one selects and evaluates the content—but some of the analysis of journalists' work actually tells a positive story. In a study of the A sections and section fronts of three agenda-setting newspapers—the *Washington Post*, *New York Times* and *Los Angeles Times*—researchers at Bowling Green State University in Ohio found a remarkable degree of balance.

Despite frequent complaints that the media have been unfair (particularly from the Clinton camp), Clinton and Obama received roughly equal number of "positive" and "negative" headlines from the three papers during the period studied (from Labor Day through the Super Tuesday primaries in early February). About 35 percent of the headlines for Obama were positive and 27 percent were negative. Clinton received 31 percent positive and 31 percent negative. The balance of stories was judged to be either mixed (with positive and negative elements) or neutral.

Just as important, perhaps, is that Clinton's coverage wasn't "gendered" in the traditional way. That is, it didn't emphasize her clothing and appearance, something that candidates such as Patricia Schroeder and Elizabeth Dole faced in earlier campaigns. This may reflect the fact that Clinton is one of the best-known women in the world, with a long history in the spotlight. Nevertheless, the coverage tended to focus on her campaign and policy questions, the study found.

TV coverage may be a different story, acknowledges Melissa K. Miller, one of the study's two principal investigators, but that was beyond her scope, "I think when you systematically study press coverage in this manner, in which you're looking at hundreds if not thousands of headlines, it may give a different impression than a person sitting down in front of the TV for the evening news."

A similar analysis of the *Chicago Tribune* in March by the paper's public editor, Timothy J. McNulty, found that Obama was cited first in 93 front-page stories in the past year, compared with 80 for Clinton and 39 for McCain. Obama also led in front-page photographs (40), compared with Clinton (34) and McCain (21). A clear bias for Obama? Not exactly. "Those who see a disparity in coverage of Republicans versus Democrats are, of course, absolutely correct," McNulty wrote. "Much more space has been devoted to the ongoing struggle between Hillary Clinton and Barack Obama than to McCain because the decision regarding the Republican presidential nominee seems settled."

Which leads to:

NOT ALL CANDIDATES, NOR ALL OF THE NEWS, ARE CREATED EQUAL.

It's unrealistic, even undesirable, to expect the candidates to receive roughly the same number of stories or minutes of air-time. As McNulty pointed out, there were perfectly valid reasons why the *Tribune* would write more about Obama than Clinton or McCain. For one thing, Obama is a former community organizer and state senator from Chicago, making him the Trib's hometown candidate. What's more, he was the Democratic frontrurmer in a tight, hard-fought race. For another, not all of the coverage he received was favorable: The *Tribune* broke a number of stories about Obama's ties to Tony Rezko and covered his relationship with Rev. Wright, another Chicagoan. No doubt the Obama campaign would have preferred fewer stories about "Bittergate" or his bowling skills.

The mistake, says the *Globe*'s Milligan, is "confusing fairness with balance," when balance means equal criticism of all the candidates. "If we have fewer so-called criticisms of Obama's record, I think much of it has to do with the fact that his record is simply much shorter, and we didn't start looking at it until he ran for president," she observes. "We don't have Obama's daily schedules for eight years. . . . And we don't have seven and a half years of Obama Senate votes to scour," because he's been in the Senate just over three years.

So what's a poor, misunderstood news media monolith supposed to do to win back its public esteem and fading credibility? Perhaps the future lies in the past, in going back to the basics taught in beginning journalism class.

"The best we can do is to try and play it straight and get the facts out as best we can," says Dan Balz.

Says Jerry Lindsley: "I hate to simplify this too much, but people are looking for a balanced presentation of ideas. They want two sides, if there are two sides. People think it's not that difficult to present both sides. Keep your personal biases at home."

To which Lichter has a three-word reply: Not gonna happen. Despite efforts to hold on to textbook notions of "objective" reporting, he says, journalistic norms have been in flux for several decades, driven by technological, economic and historic forces. The future promises only more of this. Instead of straightforward descriptive reporting, he says, the news will become more like what it has been becoming for years: More interpretive, more personal, more subjective and more opinionated. "You can't put this genie back in its bottle—there never was a bottle," he says. "There's going to be a diffusion of viewpoints. People are going to find it easier than ever to find one viewpoint they like and will stick with that."

If so, it augurs one terrifying possibility. All those complaints about bias you've been hearing lately? You haven't heard anything yet.

The Myth Of Objectivity[*]

By Evan Thomas
Newsweek, March 10, 2008

She tried to make a joke of it. At the debate in Cleveland last week, Hillary Clinton brought up a "Saturday Night Live" skit about journalists fawning over Barack Obama at a mock debate. "Maybe we should ask Barack if he's comfortable and needs another pillow," said Clinton. Humor is often a substitute for anger, and if Clinton wasn't all that funny, maybe it is because she is sore at the press for seeming to go easier on her opponent. She has a point, but the truth about the media and the campaign cannot be caricatured simply as the deification of Obama and the hounding of Clinton.

The pols and the people invest the press with great power. Conspiracies abound. Right-wing talk-show hosts love to go on about the liberal media establishment. Lefty commentators accuse the press of rolling over for George W. Bush before the invasion of Iraq. Politicians of all stripes accuse the press of being unfair, even cruel. Sometimes we are. On the day Vice President George H.W. Bush announced for the presidency in October 1987, he watched as his 28-year-old daughter, Doro, wept when she picked up *Newsweek*'s cover story that week, picturing Bush driving his speedboat under the cover line *Fighting the 'Wimp Factor.'* Bush was, understandably, furious. The phrase "wimp factor" came from Bush's own pollster, and we said he was fighting it, but we nevertheless left the impression that we were calling the vice president a wimp. In the end, the story had little impact because voters already understood that Bush, a World War II hero, was plenty tough. He was elected president the next year.

Certainly, there are editors and publishers who would like to be kingmakers, or just kings. From William Randolph Hearst to Henry Luce to Rupert Murdoch, press barons have sought to leave their personal stamp, if not change the course of history. But for the vast majority of media, the reality is much more mundane; the press's impact on elections, as well as most other human events, is murky.

The mainstream media (the "MSM" the bloggers love to rail against) are prejudiced, but not ideologically. The press's real bias is for conflict. Editors, even ones who marched in antiwar demonstrations during the Vietnam era, have a weakness for war, the ultimate conflict. Inveterate gossips and snoops, journalists also share a yen for scandal, preferably sexual. But mostly they are looking for narratives that reveal something of character. It is the human drama that most compels our attention.

Politicians have long known how to go over the heads of the press to the public. Had the voting franchise been restricted to reporters, neither Richard Nixon nor Ronald Reagan would have been elected president. Much of the Fourth Estate regarded Nixon as a thinly packaged autocrat, Reagan as a dumb nuclear cowboy. Both presidents were re-elected in landslides. Old media's political power, such as it was, has been weakened further by new media. The fund-raising power and viral reach of the Internet are far more crucial to the fortunes of a presidential candidate than sitting around eating cookies with The *Washington Post*'s editorial board.

The need to sell newspapers or win over advertisers is real and getting more pressing in an age of declining financial fortunes, but such pressures almost never affect news decisions. (If they did, there would be less political or foreign coverage, which is plentiful and is the subject of many of the criticisms leveled at the MSM. Trust us, advertisers are not eager to underwrite coverage of wars, often for fear of being associated with controversial topics.) Anyone visiting the morning meetings of the editors at most newsmagazines, major newspapers or news networks would hear a discussion of what's new, what's interesting and what's important—not what's going to make money for the publisher or owner.

A recurring rap against the press is that it lacks objectivity. The criticism is fair, in the sense that it is almost impossible to be completely objective. Subjectivity always creeps into the choices made by reporters and editors on what to include or what to emphasize in a story. News people are all too human, and sometimes they are not even aware of their biases. But on the whole, the mainstream press does try, with imperfect results, to be fair. The big news organizations are not at all relaxed about getting it wrong. Big mistakes—fraud, plagiarism, outright deceit—can kill careers.

Much of the suspicion of press bias comes from two assumptions that are commonplace, if contradictory. The first is that reporters are out to get their subjects. The second is that the press is too close to its subjects—in the parlance of journalists, "in the tank." The press has been guilty of both sins at various times. Examining the way the pendulum swings between these poles—between fawning and negativity—is a useful way of understanding how the press operates. Rare is the reporter who can be both an insider and outsider (Ben Bradlee, executive editor of The *Washington Post* from 1968 to 1991, comes to mind). Public officials tend to dislike journalists, but are forced to deal with them. As Lyndon Johnson once said, he would rather have someone "inside the tent pissing out than outside pissing in."

There was a time, in the years of the early cold war, when the press was too cozy with high government officials. The great Washington columnist Walter Lippmann would visit the Oval Office to give the president his thoughts for a speech. Then Lippmann would write a column praising the speech. Reporters favored with leaks from J. Edgar Hoover's FBI were known as "F.O.B.s"—Friends of Bureau. They never reported that Hoover was blackmailing politicians and bugging civil-rights leaders. At fancy Georgetown dinner parties, CIA officials hobnobbed with columnist Joseph Alsop, knowing that their secrets—coup plots, black ops—were safe with their social peer and fellow patriot.

Then came Vietnam and Watergate and a golden age for muckraking. President Johnson lied to the press so often that the "credibility gap" was born. Uncovering Nixon's misdeeds made movie heroes out of two young *Washington Post* city-desk reporters, Bob Woodward and Carl Bernstein. Suddenly it was cool to become a journalist, cooler still to be an investigative journalist. Newspapers began cranking out multipart series that were unreadable and often proved little (while insinuating a lot), but won the occasional prize. A giant scandal machine took over Washington, exposing wrongdoing and keeping politicians honest, but also frightening them from public service or punishing them for peccadilloes. The nadir may have been the Gary Condit-intern scandal in the spring and summer of 2001, during which the national press corps spent weeks hounding an obscure congressman for a murder he did not commit—though he did admit to an affair (according to later news reports) and, at first, allowed his staff to deny it.

After 9/11, the scandal machine shut down—for a time. Journalists were dealing again with questions of war and peace, and it seemed, for the moment at least, that the profession was ennobled by crisis. Then came Iraq. Some big-time journalists (a) were scared that Al Qaeda would attack their homes, New York and Washington, and (b) bought into the idea, albeit with misgivings, that toppling Saddam Hussein would make the country safer.

Burned by the WMD fiasco, most news organizations took up the cudgels again. Defying a personal plea from President Bush, The *New York Times* exposed extensive electronic eavesdropping on citizens in the war on terror. While controversial, the decision to reveal the eavesdropping program was in the public interest. Much more questionable was the *Times*'s later decision to publicize how intelligence officials tapped into a bank clearinghouse in Europe to follow terrorist money. The article gave terrorists all the warning they needed to avoid such money transfers, while the spying program had been authorized by Congress. The *Times*'s justification for such a damaging revelation was that the paper was guarding against a potential abuse of power.

There is a tendency among politicians to blame all their woes on the press. Certainly Hillary Clinton feels aggrieved, though part of the problem with Clinton's critique is that her life in politics is so much longer and more controversial than Obama's that there is simply more to examine: it is the rare presidential contender, for instance, who is married to a buckraking former president who lobs grenades at the first plausible African-American candidate. (Jay Carson, a Clinton spokesman, says: "Campaigns are supposed to be a test, and the press is to some extent the people who administer that test . . . There's certainly one candidate who's had their record scrubbed in the Democratic Party.") Al Gore was bitter that the traveling press corps fell for George W. Bush's fraternity-brother charm during the 2000 race, and has since lamented that the press lacks the capacity to understand and explain technical concepts, like health care or global warming. Yet Gore himself was able to go around and over the press, to use the airwaves and the Internet, to issue his timely jeremiads and win a Nobel Prize—and an Oscar for "An Inconvenient Truth."

It is true that reporters are susceptible to flash and charm; like most cynics, they are romantics in disguise. JFK and the early Bill Clinton were bound to get better press than insecure Richard Nixon or earnest Al Gore (who for some reason hides a raucous sense of humor). Right now, Obama and John McCain are popular with reporters. But if the usual laws of press physics apply, the media will turn on both men before Election Day. The blogs and the talk-show hosts will rant. The voters will take it all in (or not). And then make up their own minds.

Red Media, Blue Media[*]

Evidence for a Political Litmus Test in Online News Readership

By Shanto Iyengar and Richard Morin
The Washington Post, May 3, 2006

Thirty years ago, you had to visit the public library to read something other than your local newspaper. Today, thanks to information technology, newspapers, radio and television networks the world over are no more that a keystroke away. Does this dramatic expansion of available news outlets mean that Americans—and others worldwide—will be exposed to a more diverse "marketplace of ideas," gain familiarity with new points of view and become more tolerant? Or will consumers stick with their preferred (politically compatible) news sources while screening out those sites offering unfamiliar or disagreeable information and perspectives?

As yet, there is little evidence to indicate that consumers apply a political litmus test in deciding which news sources to use. We designed this study to find out whether people do in fact prefer news reports from sources that they believe to be sympathetic or compatible with their views. We observed whether attention to the identical news story was increased or decreased when the story was attributed to Fox News, NPR, CNN or the BBC. The results demonstrate considerable polarization in exposure to news. Republicans have distinct preferences for particular news sources (they go to Fox and avoid NPR and CNN). Democrats avoid Fox but divide their attention between CNN and NPR. When the news focuses on controversial issues, partisans are especially likely to screen out sources they consider opposed to their political views. The study design was as follows: Using the MSNBC daily news feed (which includes news reports from a variety of sources), we randomly assigned news stories (for purposes of the study) to one of four sources—Fox, NPR, CNN, or BBC. Participants were provided a brief headline accompanied by the logo of the news organization and asked to indicate which of the four reports displayed on the screen they would like to read. (They could also click a "can't say" box.) They repeated this task across six different news categories—American politics, the war in Iraq, "race in America," crime, travel, and sports. We also included a baseline or control condition in which all source logos were deleted; here participants could only choose between the reports based on the text of the headlines.

All other aspects of the presentation were equalized across the different news organizations. For instance, the placement of a particular story or source on the screen was randomized so that no particular news source gained from being the first or last on the screen.

We were able to supplement the "drop-in" sample with a representative national sample of adult Americans made available through the market research firm of Polimetrix, headed by Stanford professor Douglas Rivers. The Polimetrix sampling methodology is available at http://www.polimetrix.com. The use of a second sample permitted us to compare the media choices of *Post* readers with those of the population at large. This was especially important given the paucity of Republicans (only 11 percent) in the *Post*'s participant pool. The PMX sample, by contrast, was 33 percent Republican.

Our main expectation was that we would find a stronger demand among Republicans and those with conservative political views when reports were assigned to the Fox condition, while readers on the left would be more interested in stories assigned to CNN or NPR. Since the BBC is a foreign news source with a well-deserved reputation for independent journalism, we expected similar preferences for the BBC label among Democrats, Republicans and non-partisans alike. We further expected that the effects of the source manipulation on news story selection would be strong for political topics where partisan divisions are intense, but would have little impact on neutral topics such as travel and sports. As shown in Figure 1 and Figure 2, this is precisely what we found—the divide between Republicans and Democrats proved considerable when news stories dealt with national politics or the war in Iraq, but was relatively small when the news turned to travel or sports. Even though the partisan divide is greater in the case of hard news, it does

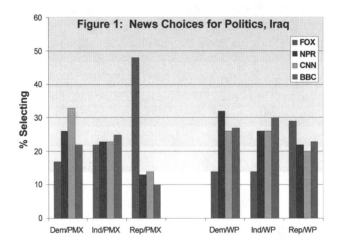

Figure 1: News Choices for Politics, Iraq

not disappear entirely for non-political subjects. Republicans prefer Fox News, even when reading about possible vacation destinations.

Despite the fact that Fox won the Republican "vote" in both samples, there were clear differences in the intensity of preference. While Republicans in the national sample preferred Fox by a landslide margin, Republicans among *Post* readers were more willing to look elsewhere, resulting in a narrow (although still statistically significant) margin for Fox.

The Democrats did not converge on a single source, but tended to divide their selections between CNN and NPR. Nationwide, Democrats opted for CNN; in the Post sample, they preferred NPR. In one important respect, however, the two groups of Democrats behaved similarly—they demonstrated an equally strong aversion to Fox. Finally, independents lived up to their designation and revealed no particular source preference, although among those in the *Post* sample, they were just as averse as the Democrats to offerings from Fox. A more pointed indicator of partisan preference is whether respondents perceive media treatment of President George W. Bush as biased. We asked respondents to indicate whether they thought the news media were either insufficiently or overly critical of the president. As shown in Figure 3, beliefs about the media's treatment of President Bush is a very powerful determinant of the overall preference for Fox news reports. (These results are based only on the hard news categories.) Fox loyalists come disproportionately from those who think the media are too tough on President Bush. On the other side, people who feel that the media should provide more critical coverage of the administration are much more likely to select NPR and CNN over FOX.

As a final indicator of the relationship between partisan preference and news selection, we present results comparing story selection rates with and without source labels (see Figure 4). As part of the design, one-quarter of the study participants were provided with the news reports without source labels. Therefore, we were able to compare the fraction of the study participants who selected the same story

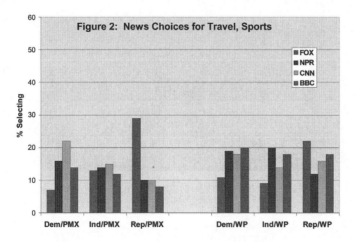

when it was either unlabelled, or attributed either to Fox News or CNN and NPR. (The small number of Republicans made it difficult to carry out this story-level analysis in the Post sample, hence we limit this analysis to the national sample.) In this analysis we are comparing hit rates for the same story; any difference in the number of people selecting the story can only be attributed to the presence or absence of the source label.

Figure 4 provides considerable evidence of political selectivity: the very same news story on crime or Iraq or politics or racial issues attracts a different audience when labeled as a Fox or NPR report. The effects of the story label proved most powerful in the case of Fox. On average, adding the Fox label to a story more than tripled the Republican "hit rate" for hard news stories! Consistent with our expectations, the effects of the Fox label were weakened for non-political news. Nonetheless, the effects of the Fox label doubled the selection rate for travel and sports stories among Republicans. While Republicans were drawn to the Fox label, they avoided CNN and NPR. On average, the probability that a Republican would select a CNN or NPR report was around 10 percent.

As for the Democrats, they were just as averse to Fox as the Republicans were to CNN and NPR. But unlike the Republicans, they did not converge on a particular news source. Although the CNN and NPR labels boosted interest among Democrats, the effects were weak. After all, the expected selection rate for any particular source is 20 percent (participants could choose one of the four reports or "can't say"). Thus, the Democratic selection rate for CNN-NPR is just slightly above the "no preference" baseline. Overall, the results suggest that Democrats are exposed to a greater range of news sources than Republicans.

Finally, independents lived up to their designation. The effects of story labeling on their selections was miniscule. Most independents had no news preferences; they typically selected the "can't say" option.

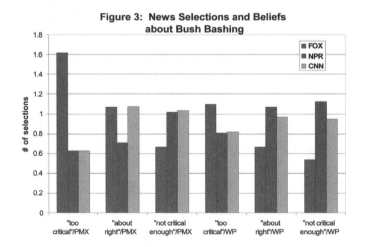

Figure 4: Effects of Story Label on Story Selection

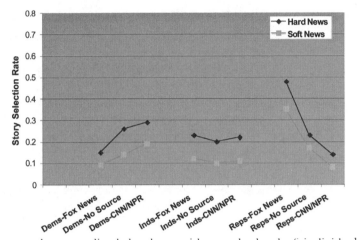

No matter how we sliced the data—either at the level of individuals or news stories—the results demonstrate that Fox News is the dominant news source for Americans whose political leanings are Republican or conservative (the results presented above are even stronger if we substitute ideology for party identification). Fox's brand advantage among Republicans is especially strong when the news deals with political subjects. The effectiveness with which Fox attracts Republicans suggests that "news with an edge"—the motto of one popular Fox News show—is no impediment to market success.

Unlike the Republican enthusiasm for Fox, Democrats showed only lukewarm preferences for CNN and NPR. Perhaps the Democrats' brand loyalty is weaker because they find CNN and NPR content insufficiently slanted to their liking. Alternatively, Democrats may be less inclined to seek out one-sided news coverage that confirms their view of the world.

One thing is certain. The importance of source labels to news consumption will only grow as technology diffuses and consumers increasingly customize their online news menus. As this trend progresses, there is the real possibility that news will no longer serve as a "social glue" that connects all Americans; instead, the very same lines that divide voters will also divide news audiences.

Public Sees Media Bias.[*]

By Ted J. Smith III
The American, July/August 2002

CBS correspondent Bernie Goldberg's book that showcases liberal bias in the media has had no discernible impact on establishment journalists. Nor should any have been expected. *Bias* is merely the latest addition to a huge body of literature—including at least 100 books and research monographs—documenting a widespread left-wing bias in the news. Yet none of it has had much effect.

Journalists and their defenders discovered long ago that such materials could usually be ignored or dismissed as the fevered ravings of right-wing zealots. On those rare occasions when a book or article breaks through to a wider audience, all that's required is a bit of damage control. First, the author is rigorously excluded from the largest popular media (which is why Goldberg has appeared only once on any of the three major television networks, though his book spent weeks at the top of the *New York Times* bestseller list). Second, in the rest of the elite media the author is subjected to personal abuse (as by Tom Shales), and endless quibbling about details of his work (as in Michael Kinsley's review). Seldom does anyone bother to respond to the substance of his argument, and in the end the attention of the public moves elsewhere.

Because the media have the power to set the terms of debate, every critic can be marginalized, every study rendered "controversial." So journalists and their apologists can always claim that media bias has not been proved. That is why Tom Goldstein, dean of the prestigious Graduate School of Journalism at Columbia University, feels free to make the astounding assertion that, while most journalists may be liberal in their views, "no study . . . has shown that the personal backgrounds and values of journalists are particularly relevant to how journalists report the news."

But there is a body of definitive evidence that proves a contrary view. Journalists like to claim that perceptions of media bias are purely a matter of perspective. They say the news is scrupulously fair and balanced, so when viewed by conservatives it appears skewed to the left, and from a liberal perspective it leans to the

* Originally published in *The American Magazine*, v.13 no.5, July/August 2002. Online at American.com.

right. To test this contention, the Center for Media and Public Affairs (CMPA) commissioned a large-scale study of public attitudes about the press. Fielded by Louis Harris and Associates in November 1996, the telephone survey sought responses to 107 questions from a representative sample of 3,004 American adults. The unusually large sample made it possible to acquire accurate information about the views of various population subgroups.

Like earlier studies, the survey found that 74 percent of Americans see either "a great deal" (30 percent) or "a fair amount" (44 percent) of "political bias in news coverage." Fully 63 percent of the public believes the news media "tend to favor one side" in "presenting the news dealing with political and social issues." But unlike most studies, this one also asked respondents to "describe the views of the news media on most matters having to do with politics," giving them the choices of "very liberal, somewhat liberal, middle-of-the-road, somewhat conservative, or very conservative." The responses are illuminating.

Among the whole public, a plurality of 43 percent described the news media as very (18 percent) or somewhat (25 percent) liberal. This compares to only 19 percent who described the media as very (6 percent) or somewhat (12 percent) conservative.

More important, the study examined 75 different subgroups of the U.S. population and found that in 73 of them more people see liberal bias than see conservative bias in the news. Even Democrats and self-described liberals came to this conclusion (see accompanying chart). This conclusively refutes the claim that perceptions of bias are solely a function of perspective.

The CMPA/Harris study also divided respondents into five levels of political participation and five levels of education. The results show a near-perfect linear progression: The higher the level of participation and education, the greater the perception of a leftist slant to the news. Among the most politically active citizens, who are presumably best able to make accurate assessments of bias, 55 percent see a liberal tilt, only 15 percent a conservative. The findings are even more striking for the educated elite (see chart).

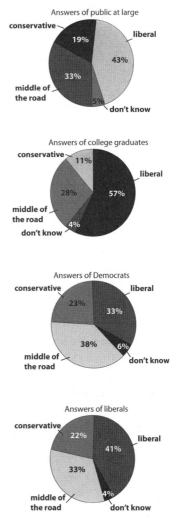

"What are the views of the news media on most matters having to do with politics?"

Answers of public at large

Answers of college graduates

Answers of Democrats

Answers of liberals

Source: Lou Harris research for Media and Public Affairs, November 1996.

The verdict is in; the People have spoken; the media are guilty as charged. The time has come to shift the debate from whether the news is biased to what can be done to correct it.

The Story Behind the Story[*]

By Mark Bowden
Atlantic Monthly, October 2009

If you happened to be watching a television news channel on May 26, the day President Obama nominated U.S. Circuit Court Judge Sonia Sotomayor to the Supreme Court, you might have been struck, as I was, by what seemed like a nifty investigative report.

First came the happy announcement ceremony at the White House, with Sotomayor sweetly saluting her elderly mother, who as a single parent had raised the prospective justice and her brother in a Bronx housing project. Obama had chosen a woman whose life journey mirrored his own: an obscure, disadvantaged beginning followed by blazing academic excellence, an Ivy League law degree, and a swift rise to power. It was a moving TV moment, well-orchestrated and in perfect harmony with the central narrative of the new Obama presidency.

But then, just minutes later, journalism rose to perform its time-honored pie-throwing role. Having been placed by the president on a pedestal, Sotomayor was now a clear target. I happened to be watching Fox News. I was slated to appear that night on one of its programs, *Hannity*, to serve as a willing foil to the show's cheerfully pugnacious host, Sean Hannity, a man who can deliver a deeply held conservative conviction on any topic faster than the speed of thought. Since the host knew what the subject matter of that night's show would be and I did not, I'd thought it best to check in and see what Fox was preoccupied with that afternoon.

With Sotomayor, of course—and the network's producers seemed amazingly well prepared. They showed a clip from remarks she had made on an obscure panel at Duke University in 2005, and then, reaching back still farther, they showed snippets from a speech she had made at Berkeley Law School in 2001. Here was this purportedly moderate Latina judge, appointed to the federal bench by a Republican president and now tapped for the Supreme Court by a Democratic one, unmasked as a Race Woman with an agenda. In one clip she announced herself as someone who believed her identity as a "Latina woman" (a redundancy, but that's what she said) made her judgment superior to that of a "white male," and in the other she all but unmasked herself as a card-carrying member of the Left Wing Conspiracy to use America's courts not just to apply and interpret the law but, in her own words, to make policy, to perform an end run around the other two branches of government and impose liberal social policies by fiat on an unsuspecting American public.

In the Duke clip, she not only stated that appellate judges make policy, she did so in a disdainful mock disavowal before a chuckling audience of apparently like-minded conspirators. "I know this is on tape and I should never say that, because we don't make law, I know," she said before being interrupted by laughter. "Okay, I know. I'm not promoting it, I'm not advocating it, I'm . . . you know," flipping her hands dismissively. More laughter.

Holy cow! I'm an old reporter, and I know legwork when I see it. Those crack journalists at Fox, better known for coloring and commenting endlessly on the news than for actually breaking it, had unearthed not one but two explosive gems, and had been primed to expose Sotomayor's darker purpose *within minutes of her nomination!* Leaving aside for the moment any question about the context of these seemingly damaging remarks—none was offered—I was impressed. In my newspaper years, I prepared my share of advance profiles of public figures, and I know the scut work that goes into sifting through a decades-long career. In the old days it meant digging through packets of yellowed clippings in the morgue, interviewing widely, searching for those moments of controversy or surprise that revealed something interesting about the subject. How many rulings, opinions, articles, legal arguments, panel discussions, and speeches had there been in the judge's long years of service? What bloodhound producer at Fox News had waded into this haystack to find these two choice needles?

Then I flipped to MSNBC, and lo! . . . they had the exact same two clips. I flipped to CNN . . . same clips. CBS . . . same clips. ABC . . . same clips. Parsing Sotomayor's 30 years of public legal work, somehow every TV network had come up with precisely the same moments! None bothered to say who had dug them up; none offered a smidgen of context. They all just accepted the apparent import of the clips, the substance of which was sure to trouble any fair-minded viewer. By the end of the day just about every American with a TV set had heard the "make policy" and "Latina woman" comments. By the end of the nightly news summaries, millions who had never heard of Sonia Sotomayor knew her not only as Obama's pick, but as a judge who felt superior by reason of her gender and ethnicity, and as a liberal activist determined to "make policy" from the federal bench. And wasn't it an extraordinary coincidence that all these great news organizations, functioning independently—because this, after all, is the advantage of having multiple news-gathering sources in a democracy—had come up with exactly the same material in advance?

They hadn't, of course. The reporting we saw on TV and on the Internet that day was the work not of journalists, but of political hit men. The snippets about Sotomayor had been circulating on conservative Web sites and shown on some TV channels for weeks. They were new only to the vast majority of us who have better things to do than vet the record of every person on Obama's list. But this is precisely what activists and bloggers on both sides of the political spectrum do, and what a conservative organization like the Judicial Confirmation Network exists to promote. The JCN had gathered an attack dossier on each of the prospective Supreme Court nominees, and had fed them all to the networks in advance.

This process—political activists supplying material for TV news broadcasts—is not new, of course. It has largely replaced the work of on-the-scene reporters during political campaigns, which have become, in a sense, perpetual. The once-quadrennial clashes between parties over the White House are now simply the way our national business is conducted. In our exhausting 24/7 news cycle, demand for timely information and analysis is greater than ever. With journalists being laid off in droves, savvy political operatives have stepped eagerly into the breach. What's most troubling is not that TV-news producers mistake their work for journalism, which is bad enough, but that young people drawn to journalism increasingly see no distinction between disinterested reporting and hit-jobbery. The very smart and capable young men (more on them in a moment) who actually dug up and initially posted the Sotomayor clips both originally described themselves to me as part-time, or aspiring, journalists.

The attack that political operatives fashioned from their work was neither unusual nor particularly effective. It succeeded in shaping the national debate over her nomination for weeks, but more serious assessments of her record would demolish the caricature soon enough, and besides, the Democrats have a large majority in the Senate; her nomination was approved by a vote of 68–31. The incident does, however, illustrate one consequence of the collapse of professional journalism. Work formerly done by reporters and producers is now routinely performed by political operatives and amateur ideologues of one stripe or another, whose goal is not to educate the public but to win. This is a trend not likely to change.

Writing in 1960, the great press critic A. J. Liebling, noting the squeeze on his profession, fretted about the emergence of the one-newspaper town:

> The worst of it is that each newspaper disappearing below the horizon carries with it, if not a point of view, at least a potential emplacement for one. A city with one newspaper, or with a morning and an evening paper under one ownership, is like a man with one eye, and often the eye is glass.

Liebling, who died in 1963, was spared the looming prospect of the no-newspaper town. There is, of course, the Internet, which he could not have imagined. Its enthusiasts rightly point out that digital media are in nearly every way superior to paper and ink, and represent, in essence, an upgrade in technology. But those giant presses and barrels of ink and fleets of delivery trucks were never what made newspapers invaluable. What gave newspapers their value was the mission and promise of journalism—the hope that someone was getting paid to wade into the daily tide of manure, sort through its deliberate lies and cunning half-truths, and tell a story straight. There is a reason why newspaper reporters, despite polls that show consistently low public regard for journalists, are the heroes of so many films. The reporter of lore was not some blue blood or Ivy League egghead, beholden to society's powerful interests, be they corporate, financial, or political. We liked our newsmen to be Everymen—shoe-leather intellectuals, cynical, suspicious, and streetwise like Humphrey Bogart in *Deadline—U.S.A.* or Jimmy Stewart in *The Philadelphia Story* or Robert Redford and Dustin Hoffman in *All the President's Men.* The Internet is now replacing Everyman with every man. Anyone with a keyboard or cell phone can report, analyze, and pull a chair up to the national debate. If freedom of the press belongs to those who own one, today that is everyone. The city with one eye (glass or no) has been replaced by the city with a million eyes. This is wonderful on many levels, and is why the tyrants of the world are struggling, with only partial success, to control the new medium. But while the Internet may be the ultimate democratic tool, it is also demolishing the business model that long sustained newspapers and TV's network-news organizations. Unless someone quickly finds a way to make disinterested reporting pay, to compensate the modern equivalent of the ink-stained wretch (the carpal-tunnel curmudgeon?), the Web may yet bury Liebling's cherished profession.

Who, after all, is willing to work for free?

Morgen Richmond, for one—the man who actually found the snippets used to attack Sotomayor. He is a partner in a computer-consulting business in Orange County, California, a father of two, and a native of Canada, who defines himself, in part, as a political conservative. He spends some of his time most nights in a second-floor bedroom/office in his home, after his children and wife have gone to bed, cruising the Internet looking for ideas and information for his blogging. "It's more of a hobby than anything else," he says. His primary outlet is a Web site called VerumSerum.com, which was co-founded by his friend John Sexton. Sexton is a Christian conservative who was working at the time for an organization called Reasons to Believe, which strives, in part, to reconcile scientific discovery and theory with the apparent whoppers told in the Bible. Sexton is, like Richmond, a young father, living in Huntington Beach. He is working toward a master's degree at Biola University (formerly the Bible Institute of Los Angeles), and is a man of opinion. He says that even as a youth, long before the Internet, he would corner his friends and make them listen to his most recent essay. For both Sexton and Richmond, Verum Serum is a labor of love, a chance for them to flex their desire to report and comment, to add their two cents to the national debate. Both see themselves as somewhat unheralded conservative thinkers in a world captive to misguided liberalism and prey to an overwhelmingly leftist mainstream media, or MSM, composed of journalists who, like myself, write for print publications or work for big broadcast networks and are actually paid for their work.

Richmond started researching Sotomayor after ABC News Washington correspondent George Stephanopoulos named her as the likely pick back on March 13.

The work involved was far less than I'd imagined, in part because the Internet is such an amazing research tool, but mostly because Richmond's goal was substantially easier to achieve than a journalist's. For a newspaper reporter, the goal in researching any profile is to arrive at a deeper understanding of the subject. My own motivation, when I did it, was to present not just a smart and original picture of the person, but a fair picture. In the quaint protocols of my ancient newsroom career, the editors I worked for would have accepted nothing less; if they felt a story needed more detail or balance, they'd brusquely hand it back and demand more effort. Richmond's purpose was fundamentally different. He figured, rightly, that anyone Obama picked who had not publicly burned an American flag would likely be confirmed, and that she would be cheered all the way down this lubricated chute by the Obama-loving MSM. To his credit, Richmond is not what we in the old days called a "thumbsucker," a lazy columnist who rarely stirs from behind his desk, who for material just reacts to the items that cross it. (This defines the vast majority of bloggers.) Richmond is actually determined to add something new to the debate.

"The goal is to develop original stories that attract attention," he told me. "I was consciously looking for something that would resonate."

But not just anything resonant. Richmond's overarching purpose was to damage Sotomayor, or at least to raise questions about her that would trouble his readers, who are mostly other conservative bloggers. On most days, he says, his stuff on Verum Serum is read by only 20 to 30 people. If any of them like what they see, they link to it or post the video on their own, larger Web sites.

Richmond began his reporting by looking at university Web sites. He had learned that many harbor little-seen recordings and transcripts of speeches made by public figures, since schools regularly sponsor lectures and panel discussions with prominent citizens, such as federal judges. Many of the events are informal and unscripted, and can afford glimpses of public figures talking unguardedly about their ideas, their life, and their convictions. Many are recorded and archived. Using Google, Richmond quickly found a list of such appearances by Sotomayor, and the first one he clicked on was the video of the 2005 panel discussion at Duke University Law School. Sotomayor and two other judges, along with two Duke faculty members, sat behind a table before a classroom filled with students interested in applying for judicial clerkships. The video is 51 minutes long and is far from riveting. About 40 minutes into it, Richmond says, he was only half listening, multitasking on his home computer, when laughter from the sound track caught his ear. He rolled back the video and heard Sotomayor utter the line about making policy, and then jokingly disavow the expression.

"What I found most offensive about it was the laughter," he says. "What was the joke? . . . Here was a sitting appellate judge in a room full of law students, treating the idea that she was making policy or law from the bench as laughable." He recognized it as a telling in-joke that his readers would not find funny.

Richmond posted the video snippet on YouTube on May 2, and then put it up with a short commentary on Verum Serum the following day, questioning whether

Sotomayor deserved to be considered moderate or bipartisan, as she had been characterized. "I'm not so sure this is going to fly," he wrote, and then invited readers to view the video. He concluded with sarcasm: "So she's a judicial activist . . . I'm sure she is a moderate one though! Unbelievable. With a comment like this I only hope that conservatives have the last laugh if she gets the nomination."

A number of larger conservative Web sites, notably Volokh.com (the Volokh Conspiracy, published by UCLA law professor Eugene Volokh) and HotAir.com (published by conservative commentator Michelle Malkin), picked up the video, and on May 4 it was aired on television for the first time, by Sean Hannity.

On Malkin's Web site, Richmond had come across a short, critical reference to a speech Sotomayor had given at Berkeley Law School, in which, according to Malkin, the prospective Supreme Court nominee said "she believes it is appropriate for a judge to consider their 'experiences as women and people of color' in their decision making, which she believes should 'affect our decisions.'"

Malkin told me that her "conservative source" for the tidbit was privileged. She used the item without checking out the actual speech, which is what Richmond set out to find. He had some trouble because Malkin had placed the speech in 2002 instead of 2001, but he found it—the Honorable Mario G. Olmos Law & Cultural Diversity Memorial Lecture—in the Berkeley Law School's *La Raza Law Journal*, bought it, and on May 5 posted the first detailed account of it on his blog. He ran large excerpts from it, and highlighted in bold the now infamous lines: "I would hope that a wise Latina woman with the richness of her experiences would more often than not reach a better conclusion than a white male who hasn't lived that life."

Richmond then commented:

> To be fair, I do want to note that the statement she made . . . is outrageous enough that it may have in fact been a joke. Although since it's published "as-is" in a law journal I'm not sure she is entitled to the benefit of the doubt on this. The text certainly does not indicate that it was said in jest. I have only a lay-person's understanding of law and judicial history, but I suspect the judicial philosophy implied by these statements is probably pretty typical amongst liberal judges. Personally, I wish it seemed that she was actually really trying to meet the judicial ideal of impartiality, and her comments about making a difference are a concern as this does not seem to be an appropriate focus for a member of the judiciary. I look forward to hopefully seeing some additional dissection and analysis of these statements by others in the conservative legal community.

The crucial piece of Richmond's post, Sotomayor's "wise Latina woman" comment, was then picked up again by other sites, and was soon being packaged with the Duke video as Exhibits A and B in the case against Sonia Sotomayor. Richmond told me that he was shocked by the immediate, widespread attention given to his work, and a little startled by the levels of outrage it provoked. "I found her comments more annoying than outrageous, to be honest," he said.

In both instances, Richmond's political bias made him tone-deaf to the context and import of Sotomayor's remarks. Bear in mind that he was looking not simply to understand the judge, but to expose her supposed hidden agenda.

Take the Duke panel first: most of the video, for obvious reasons, held little interest for Richmond. My guess is that you could fit the number of people who have actually watched the whole thing into a Motel Six bathtub. Most of the talk concerned how to make your application for a highly competitive clerkship stand out. Late in the discussion, a student asked the panel to compare clerking at the district-court (or trial-court) level and clerking at the appellate level. Sotomayor replied that clerks serving trial judges are often asked to rapidly research legal questions that develop during a trial, and to assist the judge in applying the law to the facts of that particular case. The appellate courts, on the other hand, are in the business of making rulings that are "precedential," she said, in that rulings at the appellate level serve as examples, reasons, or justifications for future proceedings in lower courts. She went on to make the ostensibly controversial remark that students who planned careers in academia or public-interest law ought to seek a clerkship at the appellate level, because that's where "policy is made."

This is absolutely true, in the sense she intended: precedential decisions, by definition, make *judicial* policy. They provide the basic principles that guide future rulings. But both Sotomayor and her audience were acutely aware of how charged the word *policy* has become in matters concerning the judiciary—conservatives accuse liberal judges, not without truth, of trying to set *national* policy from the bench. This accusation has become a rallying cry for those who believe that the Supreme Court justices should adhere strictly to the actual language and original intent of the Constitution, instead of coloring the law with their own modish theories to produce such social experiments as school desegregation, *Miranda* warnings, abortions on demand, and so forth. The polite laughter that caught Richmond's ear was recognition by the law students that the judge had inadvertently stepped in a verbal cow pie. She immediately recognized what she had done, expressed mock horror at being caught doing so on tape, and then pronounced a jocular and exaggerated mea culpa, like a scoring runner in a baseball game tiptoeing back out onto the diamond to touch a base that he might have missed. Sotomayor went on to explain in very precise terms how and why decisions at the appellate level have broader intellectual implications than those at the lower level. It is where, she said, "the law is percolating."

Seen in their proper context, these comments would probably not strike anyone as noteworthy. If anything, they showed how sensitive Sotomayor and everyone else in the room had become to fears of an "activist court."

A look at the full "Latina woman" speech at Berkeley reveals another crucial misinterpretation.

To his credit, Richmond posted as much of the speech as copyright law allows, attempting to present the most important sentence in context. But he still missed the point. Sotomayor's argument was not that she sought to use her position to further minority interests, or that her gender and background made her superior to a white male. Her central argument was that the sexual, racial, and ethnic makeup of the legal profession has in fact historically informed the application of law, despite the efforts of individual lawyers and judges to rise above their personal stories—as Sotomayor noted she labors to do. Her comment about a "wise Latina woman" making a better judgment than a "white male who hasn't lived that life" referred specifically to cases involving racial and sexual discrimination. "Whether born from experience or inherent physiological or cultural differences . . . our gender and national origins may and will make a difference in our judging," she said. This is not a remarkable insight, nor is it even arguable. Consider, say, how an African-American Supreme Court justice might have viewed the *Dred Scott* case, or how a female judge—Sotomayor cited this in the speech—might have looked upon the argument, advanced to oppose women's suffrage, that females are "not capable of reasoning or thinking logically." The presence of blacks and women in the room inherently changes judicial deliberation. She said that although white male judges have been admirably able on occasion to rise above cultural prejudices, the progress of racial minorities and women in the legal profession has directly coincided with greater judicial recognition of their rights. Once again, her point was not that this progress was the result of deliberate judicial activism, but that it was a natural consequence of fuller minority and female participation.

One of her central points was that all judges are, to an extent, defined by their identity and experience, whether they like it or not.

"I can and do aspire to be greater than the sum total of my experiences," she said, "but I accept my limitations."

Richmond seems a bright and fair-minded fellow, but he makes no bones about his political convictions or the purpose of his research and blogging. He has some of the skills and instincts of a reporter but not the motivation or ethics. Any news organization that simply trusted and aired his editing of Sotomayor's remarks, as every one of them did, was abdicating its responsibility to do its own reporting. It was airing propaganda. There is nothing wrong with reporting propaganda, per se, so long as it is labeled as such. None of the TV reports I saw on May 26 cited VerumSerum.com as the source of the material, which disappointed but did not surprise Richmond and Sexton.

Both found the impact of their volunteer effort exciting. They experienced the heady feeling of every reporter who discovers that the number of people who actually seek out new information themselves, even people in the news profession, is vanishingly small. Show the world something it hasn't seen, surprise it with something new, and you fundamentally alter its understanding of things. I have experienced this throughout my career, in ways large and small. I remember the first time I did, very early on, when I wrote a magazine profile of a promising Baltimore County politician named Ted Venetoulis, who was preparing a run for governor of Maryland. I wrote a long story about the man, examining his record as county executive and offering a view of him that included both praise and criticism. I was 25 years old and had never written a word about Maryland politics. I was not especially knowledgeable about the state or the candidates, and the story was amateurish at best. Yet in the months of campaigning that followed, I found snippets from that article repeatedly quoted in the literature put out by Venetoulis and by his opponents. My story was used both to promote him and to attack him.

To a large and slightly appalling extent, the points I made framed the public's perception of the candidate, who, as it happened, lost.

Several hours of Internet snooping by Richmond at his upstairs computer wound up shaping the public's perception of Sonia Sotomayor, at least for the first few weeks following her nomination. Conservative critics used the snippets to portray her as a racist and liberal activist, a picture even Richmond now admits is inaccurate. "She's really fairly moderate, compared to some of the other candidates on Obama's list," he says. "Given that conservatives are not going to like any Obama pick, she really wasn't all that bad." He felt many of the Web sites and TV commentators who used his work inflated its significance well beyond his own intent. But he was not displeased.

"I was amazed," he told me.

For his part, Sexton says: "It is a beautiful thing to live in this country. It's overwhelming and fantastic, really, that an ordinary citizen, with just a little bit of work, can help shape the national debate. Once you get a taste of it, it's hard to resist."

I would describe their approach as post-journalistic. It sees democracy, by definition, as perpetual political battle. The blogger's role is to help his side. Distortions and inaccuracies, lapses of judgment, the absence of context, all of these things matter only a little, because they are committed by both sides, and tend to come out a wash. Nobody is actually right about anything, no matter how certain they pretend to be. The truth is something that emerges from the cauldron of debate. No, not the truth: *victory*, because winning is way more important than being right. Power is the highest achievement. There is nothing new about this. But we never used to mistake it for journalism. Today it is rapidly replacing journalism, leading us toward a world where all information is spun, and where all "news" is unapologetically propaganda.

In this post-journalistic world, the model for all national debate becomes the trial, where adversaries face off, representing opposing points of view. We accept the harshness of this process because the consequences in a courtroom are so stark; trials are about assigning guilt or responsibility for harm. There is very little wiggle room in such a confrontation, very little room for compromise—only innocence or degrees of guilt or responsibility. But isn't this model unduly harsh for political debate? Isn't there, in fact, middle ground in most public disputes? Isn't the art of politics finding that middle ground, weighing the public good against factional priorities? Without journalism, the public good is viewed only through a partisan lens, and politics becomes blood sport.

Television loves this, because it is dramatic. Confrontation is all. And given the fragmentation of news on the Internet and on cable television, Americans increasingly choose to listen only to their own side of the argument, to bloggers and commentators who reinforce their convictions and paint the world only in acceptable, comfortable colors. Bloggers like Richmond and Sexton, and TV hosts like Hannity, preach only to the choir. Consumers of such "news" become all the more entrenched in their prejudices, and ever more hostile to those who disagree. The other side is no longer the honorable opposition, maybe partly right; but rather always wrong, stupid, criminal, even downright evil. Yet even in criminal courts, before assigning punishment, judges routinely order presentencing reports, which attempt to go beyond the clash of extremes in the courtroom to a more nuanced, disinterested assessment of a case. Usually someone who is neither prosecution nor defense is assigned to investigate. In a post-journalistic society, there is no disinterested voice. There are only the winning side and the losing side.

There's more here than just an old journalist's lament over his dying profession, or over the social cost of losing great newspapers and great TV-news operations. And there's more than an argument for the ethical superiority of honest, disinterested reporting over advocacy. Even an eager and ambitious political blogger like Richmond, because he is drawn to the work primarily out of political conviction, not curiosity, is less likely to experience the pleasure of finding something new, or of arriving at a completely original, unexpected insight, one that surprises even himself. He is missing out on the great fun of speaking wholly for himself, without fear or favor. This is what gives reporters the power to stir up trouble wherever they go. They can shake preconceptions and poke holes in presumption. They can celebrate the unnoticed and puncture the hyped. They can, as the old saying goes, afflict the comfortable and comfort the afflicted. A reporter who thinks and speaks for himself, whose preeminent goal is providing deeper understanding, aspires even in political argument to persuade, which requires at the very least being seen as fair-minded and trustworthy by those—and this is the key—who are inclined to disagree with him. The honest, disinterested voice of a true journalist carries an authority that no self-branded liberal or conservative can have. "For a country to have a great writer is like having another government," Alexander Solzhenitsyn wrote. Journalism, done right, is enormously powerful precisely because it does not seek power. It seeks truth. Those who forsake it to shill for a product or a candidate or a party or an ideology diminish their own power. They are missing the most joyful part of the job.

This is what H. L. Mencken was getting at when he famously described his early years as a *Baltimore Sun* reporter. He called it "the life of kings."

4

The 24-Hour News Cycle:
The Cable News Effect

Editor's Introduction

Over the past two decades, what constitutes the news cycle has evolved to such a degree that what it is now bears little resemblance to what it once was. In the days before the Internet and cable news networks, most people kept up with events through daily newspapers and the nightly news, perhaps with some news radio thrown in. Newspaper editions came out in either the morning or the evening, so at best there were two different versions of newspaper content each day. Nightly news broadcasts came on at the same time every evening and focused on the day's major stories. So there were three major points of news emphasis per day, each of which had its own strengths and limitations. For example, a newspaper could not include audio or video, while the nightly news, running half an hour in length, could not cover a story with the same degree of depth and analysis as a series of lengthy news articles.

With the development of the Internet and such cable channels as CNN, MSNBC, Fox News, and their affiliates, however, the news is now a 24-hour business, the deadlines are constant, and real-time reporting, or at least real-time content, is essential. Now, newspapers and on-line news organizations can post articles, video, and audio to their Web sites throughout the day, updating the material as events transpire or new information comes to light. Bloggers can break their own news or comment on what's already been reported at any hour.

Meanwhile, the cable news networks require an unending stream of content to keep viewers engaged. A slow news day does not mean any letup in pace or that there is less ground to cover. Many times, seemingly trivial or unimportant stories can, through constant repetition, take on a life of their own. Increasingly, given the high cost and time constraints of traditional shoe-leather journalism, cable news has shown a preference for commentary over coverage. This commentary most often takes the form of the opinionated anchor, be it the left-of-center Keith Olbermann on MSNBC or the conservative Glenn Beck on Fox News, who selects stories with a distinct political agenda in mind.

Dubbed the "cable news effect," the impact of the 24-hour news cycle has influenced not only how the news is consumed, but how it is reported, what stories are given top billing, and which ones are ignored. The selections contained in this chapter consider the impact of this new era in journalism, its limitations, and how it shapes the public's understanding of the larger world.

Paul Farhi, in "Cable's Clout," the first article, discusses cable's growing prominence as a news source and how it has affected the traditional interplay between the news sources of old and the public. As an example of cable's power to shape the national discourse, he cites the Reverend Jeremiah Wright controversy during the 2008 presidential campaign. As then-Senator Barack Obama's minister, Wright was known for his sometimes incendiary sermons, many of which had to do with race. Some of his more controversial statements were subsequently broadcast ad nauseam on cable television and threatened Obama's bid for the White House. "The cable networks rarely break news themselves," Farhi observes. Rather, "they tend to rely on newspapers and Web sites for that—but few campaign stories have much impact or become an important part of the campaign narrative until they get heavy play on cable."

In "A Day in the Life of the Media," an excerpt from the Project for Excellence in Journalism (PEJ)'s 2006 "State of the News Media" report, the authors chronicle the news cycle as it unfolds during the course of a single day in a variety of journalistic media, from old-style newspapers to cable news networks and emerging Web sites. They conclude that "Consuming the news continuously does not mean being better informed. There is too much repetition, and too much confusion." Moreover, they don't lobby for one journalistic form over another, declaring, "The most efficient diet means finding the right mix depending on the time of day, the nature of the news that day, and more."

Demonstrating in painful detail the downsides of the cable news effect, in the next piece, "Our Opinion: Accuracy the Victim of the 24-Hour News Cycle," the writers discuss news coverage of the recent shootings at Fort Hood, in Texas. Throughout the day, the details reported by the news media turned out to be grossly inaccurate. "Journalism's motto used to be: 'Be first but be right,'" the authors observe. "One out of two isn't enough."

Cable news networks are dominated by commentary, with networks like MSNBC associated with more liberal perspectives and Fox News Channel more conservative ones. Cynthia Littleton and Michael Learmonth, in the final piece in this chapter, "Cable News Divides to Conquer: Partisan Voices on the Rise in Election Cycle," consider why this trend developed and how it is affecting the public's relationship with the news. "What you have now," Professor Tom Hollihan tells Littleon and Learmonth, "is (all-news) networks trying to reach those people who are most interested in politics. Those are people who tend to be intensely partisan and have a take-no-prisoners attitude to politics."

Cable's Clout[*]

By Paul Farhi
American Journalism Review, August/September 2008

Chances are, most Americans knew something about Sen. Barack Obama's for-mer pastor, the Rev. Jeremiah Wright, by the middle of March. Wright, after all, had been mentioned in connection with Obama in hundreds of print, online and broadcast reports since Obama had declared his candidacy for president in Febru-ary 2007. News accounts typically described Wright as a "controversial" preacher and "fiery" orator. Early in the Illinois Democrat's campaign, a video posted on YouTube showed Wright calling America "the No. 1 killer in the world."

But it wasn't until early March that millions of people began to see just how fi-ery and controversial Wright could be. After Fox News and then ABC News aired newly acquired DVDs of Wright's more incendiary sermons—"The government gives them the drugs, builds bigger prisons, passes a three-strike law and then wants us to sing 'God Bless America.' No, no, no, God damn America!"—the story went from brushfire to raging conflagration. The Wright tapes all but took over cable news' coverage and daily discussion panels, with the sort of round-the-clock intensity that cable reserves for political scandals and celebrity deaths. By week's end, the story—really, the story about Obama's reaction to the story—had landed the Wright issue on the front page of the *Washington Post*. (Disclosure: I'm a reporter for the *Post*.)

The episode was a perfect illustration of what might be called "the cable news effect." In recent years, and particularly during the current presidential campaign, stories become much bigger deals as a result of the repetition and prominence giv-en to them by cable's big three: CNN, Fox News and MSNBC. The cable networks rarely break news themselves—they tend to rely on newspapers and Web sites for that—but few campaign stories have much impact or become an important part of the campaign narrative until they get heavy play on cable.

Cable, in other words, creates its own news wave, generating news simply by placing other sources' reporting on the agenda. The most famous example may be the nonstop controversy over the Swift Boat Veterans for Truth's allegations that Democratic presidential candidate John Kerry had distorted his military record in Vietnam. The episode began in August 2004, after the group ran a series of TV ads in battleground states. Fanned by relentless exposure on cable, the Swift Boat episode soon grew into a test of the Kerry campaign's media-management skills, one it hardly aced.

Cable networks have amplified and prolonged a series of gaffes and flaps in the current campaign, too. When Charles Black, a top adviser to Sen. John McCain, mentioned in June that a new terrorism strike on the U.S. would "certainly be a big advantage" to the Arizona Republican, the comment received just a half-sentence in its source publication, *Fortune* magazine. But Black's quote engendered several days of discussion on cable. Geraldine Ferraro's comment about the Obama campaign ("If Obama was a white man, he would not be in this position . . . ") first appeared in the Daily Breeze in Torrance, California, but sparked another long-running cable paroxysm. Obama's observation about small-town voters in Pennsylvania ("they get bitter, they cling to guns or religion or antipathy to people who aren't like them . . . ") was first reported by blogger Mayhill Fowler on The Huffington Post, but the contretemps got much wider and prolonged attention on cable. Ditto Michelle Obama's comment at a rally in February that "for the first time in my adult life I am proud of my country," and Obama adviser Samantha Power's assessment of Sen. Hillary Clinton as "a monster" during an interview with a Scottish newspaper in March.

Then there was Clinton's statement that she had come under sniper fire when she visited Bosnia as First Lady in 1996. Washingtonpost.com columnist Mary Ann Akers first reported that the comedian Sinbad, who accompanied Clinton on the USO-sponsored trip, said there was no sniper fire or any evident danger as they arrived. But the story initially received very little attention from television, and indeed Clinton subsequently upped the ante, saying in a speech that she and her party had to run for safety "with our heads down." In a column that appeared on March 22, the *Washington Post*'s Michael Dobbs fact-checked Clinton's version of events and found it to be flawed in almost every respect. Even so, Clinton didn't withdraw her account until several days later—after TV footage, showing a peaceful arrival in Bosnia, began playing on endless loops on cable and broadcast TV.

Who, or what, influences the news agenda can be a touchy topic for print reporters. For the most part, journalists at elite newspapers sniff at the notion that cable influences their editorial decisions. "I don't think there's a fixed pattern to who leads whom in this world," says Gerald Seib, executive Washington editor of the *Wall Street Journal*. Instead, Seib says, political news emerges from a complex media ecosystem involving reactions and counter-reactions among Internet (text and video) sources, broadcast and cable TV, and print.

If anything, print journalists suggest their work tends to find its way onto cable more often than the opposite. "There's a disincentive to follow what cable is talking about," says Anne Kornblut, who covers the campaign for the *Washington Post*. Topics on cable "will have been talked to death by the time we get around them. We need to look for what's new." Kornblut says this moments after appearing on CNN to talk about her story in that morning's paper about the newfound unity among the Obama and Clinton campaigns. It was her third such appearance on cable that day.

"I think the notion that mainstream publications orbit around cable is overstated," agrees Mark Leibovich, a *New York Times* political reporter. Leibovich also spent a busy day recently talking on TV about a story he'd written about the Clinton campaign's "enemies list." The story, which appeared inside the *Times*, had an almost tongue-in-cheek tone, yet it commanded ample airtime on MSNBC. The enemies list story was, in many respects, tailor-made for cable. It had everything cable demands: conflict, well-known personalities and a dramatic context (the last days of Clinton's campaign). Except for the sketchiness of the facts (the campaign officially denied that any such list existed), it might even have become cable's holy grail: the story of the day.

As CNN discovered during the first Persian Gulf War and later with the O.J. Simpson saga, all-news channels maximize and sustain their relatively small audiences not by covering many subjects throughout the day, but by focusing intently on one story. Sometimes cable's coverage of an event is so disproportionate to the rest of the news media's that it distorts the public's perception of the media agenda. In the 23 days between reality TV star Anna Nicole Smith's death and her burial in early 2007, the story dominated cable and morning broadcast TV newscasts. But other media sources gave it only passing mention. As the Project for Excellence in Journalism noted in its study of the coverage, "These findings add to the evidence of cable's fixation on one big event. But they also go beyond that. The fact that for the most part, the newspapers, Web sites, nightly network newscasts and radio news outlets treated Smith's death as a mere blip on the radar screen speaks to cable's ability to magnify an event until it feels like the only story on the entire media agenda."

For much of the past year, and certainly since January, cable's obsessive focus has been the presidential campaign. About two-thirds of cable news airtime this year has been devoted to campaign stories, a far higher fraction than any other news medium's, according to the PEJ. "Cable is hungrily searching" for a story it can hammer throughout a daily news cycle, says Mark Jurkowitz of the PEJ. "The question it asks is, 'What are they fighting about today?' Today it will be [McCain campaign official] Charbe Black. Tomorrow it will be a misstatement by someone else."

That's where cable exerts its biggest influence on the rest of the media—as an engine of reaction and response. Cable's intense and often immediate coverage of the day's big controversy forces candidates to fire back, which then compels the rest of the media to cover the response. When, for example, Hillary Clinton told the editorial board of the Argus Leader in Sioux Falls, South Dakota, in late May that it wasn't time for her to drop out of the race because "we all remember Bobby

Kennedy was assassinated in June in California," the comments were picked up online, significantly by the closely watched Drudge Report. Clinton's operatives then used cable to respond to the growing controversy Clinton's quasi-apology ("I regret that if my referencing that moment of trauma for our entire nation, and particularly for the Kennedy family, was in any way offensive") was on the air within hours, and her surrogates took to the panel programs to defend her. The next day's newspaper stories moved beyond the controversy itself and detailed the campaign's largely successful efforts at damage control.

Cable's obsession with the campaign and its ubiquitous presence also mean that candidates no longer are bound by TV's traditional deadlines—the late afternoon —to make or break news. Now they do it at the time most advantageous to them, raising or lowering a story's profile in the process. McCain made his baffled and somewhat peeved response to the *New York Times*' controversial story about his purported relationship with lobbyist Vicki Iseman at a morning press conference. By the time Brian Williams, Charles Gibson and Katie Couric reported it on the evening network newscasts, it was essentially old news. Obama's speech about race in America and his relationship with Wright, carried live on cable in March, also took place in the morning.

"Campaigns have gotten much better at manipulating the [news cycle] because cable is always there," says Elizabeth Wilner, a former political director of NBC News who is now head of public affairs at the Peter G. Peterson Foundation. "They know cable is always dying for something to cover." There's nothing the cable networks love more, she says, than to post a chyron on the screen reading, "Breaking News" or "Developing Story."

The Internet-to-cable-to-print news chain isn't new, of course, but it is many years removed from, and several times more complicated than, the old news model. A generation ago, during the pre-cable era, ABC, CBS and NBC were far more likely to "borrow" their nightly news lineups from that morning's *Washington Post, New York Times* and other top papers, says Craig Allen, associate professor at the Walter Cronkite School of Journalism at Arizona State University. "The cliché always is supported by the classic example: the CBS Evening News' near-syndication of the *Post*'s Watergate stories in the fall of 1972," he says. Another example was television's coverage of the *New York Times* exposure of the Pentagon Papers a year before that. Says Allen, "The three networks were megaphones for the best of what the elite newspapers reported. That helped give [the papers] the elite distinction" in the first place.

This is not to say that network news didn't exert its own influence. Significantly, the networks used their own polls (partnering with the likes of George Gallup and Louis Harris) to develop "horse race" campaign stories for the nightly news early on, Allen says. NBC and CBS used exit polls in the 1960 election. In turn, these polls influenced newspapers' agendas; Allen found that during the 1968 presidential primaries, the *New York Times* published more stories on polls than on that year's big campaign issue, the Vietnam War.

Campaign news was also shaped by the Sunday morning talk shows, which were much more influential than they are today, according to Allen. Elite newspapers, he says, routinely wrote stories about what was said on programs like "Meet the Press" and "Face the Nation," which then as now commanded far larger audiences than their cable descendants, such as "Hardball," "The O'Reilly Factor" and "Countdown with Keith Olbermann."

These days, Olbermann notes, a cable network doesn't wait for the morning newspaper to hit the doorstep to know what's news. Even 10 years ago, newspapers held their breaking stories until their bulldog editions, which typically were on the streets around 10 or 11 p.m. Now, the cycle is faster. MSNBC, for example, was reporting on the *Times'* lengthy investigation of McCain's relationship with a lobbyist a few minutes after the paper posted the story online, around 7:30 p.m. the day before publication of the print version.

Nevertheless, Olbermann says newspapers play a diminishing role in how he presents and comments on the news each night. "For us in particular, I don't think a newspaper story dictates our lead, or significantly shapes our entire rundown, more than once every couple of weeks," he says. Conversely, he adds, "I don't know that anything I've done here has ever dictated how newspapers have covered a specific story, but I think some of the Special Comments [Olbermann's lengthy and often angry outbursts of personal opinion] put a spotlight on big-picture issues some of the papers, and indeed most of the political figures, were not willing or able to address," such as the rights of jailed terrorism suspects.

There's something more prosaic to consider in any discussion of influence: the prominence of television in newsrooms everywhere. Is there a newsroom in America that doesn't have its TVs tuned to a news station throughout the day? At my own newspaper, an oversize flat-screen TV was recently installed in the foyer of our main newsroom, making CNN or MSNBC the first thing visitors and employees encounter when they step off the elevator. Reporters such as Kornblut pooh-pooh the significance of this, saying that TV is just one more news source, no different than having an Internet connection on one's desktop. But there may be more to it than that. "I can't dismiss the idea that there's a kind of osmosis effect," the *Times'* Leibovich says. "At our bureau, we have half a dozen political reporters with the TV on all day. Sometimes it's just background noise. But it's human nature to see Jeremiah Wright or Hillary's RFK comment on TV all day and think, 'Maybe this is something we should follow.'"

Indeed, says the PEJ's Jurkowitz, "There are dynamics at work in every newsroom, including the most prestigious and powerful and most self-satisfied, that a story needs to be addressed if enough people are talking about it."

In fact, *Post* National Editor Rajiv Chandrasekaran says his newspaper needs to stay more attuned to TV's agenda. "I can't tell you what led 'Anderson Cooper 360' or 'The O'Reilly Factor' or Olbermann last night," he says, "I can tell you what was on the front page of the *New York Times* or the *Wall Street Journal*, or what Drudge has. I do check CNN's Web site." Chandrasekaran isn't being prideful or arrogant. In fact, he says the *Post* needs to pay closer attention to TV. "We may not be devoting enough energy to understanding what people are watching and engaging with, and that we can add value to [by covering]. We should at least be cognizant of it. The people we're trying to sell the paper to are more likely to be watching some portion of cable news than reading the *New York Times*. [But] in our bubble, we're more concerned about what our print competitors are doing than TV."

Over at CNN's Washington bureau, the view is decidedly different. At his desk, David Bohrman, the network's bureau chief, can monitor 11 TV screens. The sets carry the three primary cable news channels, the local network affiliates, CNN Headline News, C-SPAN and CNBC. A set at the upper left of this array carries a special 28-screen grid of pool feeds from such venues as the White House and the Capitol. While this isn't an atypical setup for a TV news director, it's what you don't see around Bohrman's desk that's telling: stacks of newsprint. "I think the major newspapers—the *Post*, the *Times*, the *Journal*, those three—have and will continue to have a prominence in the newsroom," Bohrman says. But, he adds, "Newspapers are having a rough time right now. They don't have the immediacy of TV or the Web. They've got to figure out how to capture that, capture that sweet spot of relevance. . . . Some newspapers are still trapped in writing about yesterday."

Thanks to the competitive jolt of the Internet, Bohrman says, CNN has learned to do things faster and to get news on the air sooner to compete with the Web as a breaking-news medium. "There's much more of a deadline consciousness now at CNN than there was even five years ago," he says.

Cable's prominence and immediacy has boosted its prestige within the giant companies that own the Big Three, rivaling the nightly broadcast newscasts, Elizabeth Wilner says. In recent years "MSNBC has gained in stature within the network," given that it is always on and competes directly with the Internet for breaking news, she says. "Management and talent have taken notice. You see more evening news talent on cable, and more of what was on cable that day in the evening news. They might not admit it, but the center of gravity is shifting. Cable news is on the rise; appointment news is on the wane."

A Day in the Life of the Media[*]

By the Project for Excellence in Journalism (PEJ)
Excerpted from "The State of the News Media, 2006"

May 11, 2005 was not what most people would call an extraordinary day. A warm spell moved through the Northwest into the South. Rain pelted the Rust Belt, and it was still cold in the East.

In the capital, Congress debated the appointment of John Bolton as ambassador to the U.N. The Bush administration continued to press plans to revise Social Security. Amtrak officials tried to sort out what was causing cracks in the Acela trains between Washington and Boston. The actor Macaulay Culkin testified at Michael Jackson's molestation trial. In a small town called Zion, Ill., the police charged an ex-convict named Jerry Hobbs with murdering his 8-year-old daughter and her friend.

Abroad, a series of terrorist car bomb attacks in Iraq killed 79, the culmination of four weeks of escalating violence. North Korea claimed to have removed fuel rods from nuclear reactors that could be used for nuclear weapons. Hundreds in Afghanistan protested after reports, little noticed yet in the U.S., that interrogators at Guantanamo Bay, Cuba, had desecrated the Koran.

In 2005, Americans could turn to the widest array of media outlets in history, a combination of 19th century print outlets, 20th century radio and TV outlets, and 21st century Web sites and blogs—each of them trying to distill and order events into an account of the day.

Prior years of this report examined a representative sample month of news to get a broad picture of the tendencies, strengths and weaknesses of different media. But it was impossible to see how an individual event was covered up close, to get a feel beyond the numbers. To do that, we decided this year to monitor A Day in the Life of the News, to examine in detail what audiences got over 24 hours from a wide range of news media at the national and local level online, on radio, on television and in print.

What would Americans learn from one medium versus another, and what would they not? How do stories come and go over a few hours? As citizens make their daily news choices, where could they go for certain kinds of information versus others? To the extent that a single day offers clues, what would a sensible and varied news diet look like?

Among the findings:

- What people learn depends heavily on where they go for news. The medium may not be the message, but it no doubt influences it. In print, online and on the network evening newscasts this day, violence in Iraq, a false alarm in Washington, and protests in Afghanistan were the top stories. On cable and morning news, the trial of Michael Jackson and the Illinois murder case were played higher. On local TV and radio, weather, traffic and local crime dominated—and that was an altogether different definition of local than one finds in print. As the media fragments nowadays, consumers must choose strategically to get a complete diet. The notion of relying on a single or primary source for news—one-stop shopping—may no longer make sense.

- When audiences did encounter the same story in different places, often they heard from a surprisingly small number of sources. Every network morning show and cable program covered the story about a security scare involving President Bush by interviewing the same lone person, a security expert from Citibank.[1] (A grenade, which did not explode, had been found near the site where Bush made a speech in Tbilisi, Georgia.) The murder in Illinois was similarly covered in national broadcast news mainly by interviewing the local prosecutor. More coverage, in other words, does not always mean greater diversity of voices.

- The incremental and even ephemeral nature of what the media define as news is striking. Few of what would emerge as the top stories this day would be remembered months later—or even, a search of data bases reveals, get much coverage within a day or two. And the efforts to add context to some ongoing stories were inhibited by speed, space and journalistic formula, especially on television. Journalism has always leaned toward the transitory and incremental over the systemic—news that breaks rather than news that bends. The older part of the 24-hour-news system—cable news—seems to have exaggerated this with a fixation on immediacy. It is less clear which way the Internet leans. Some online sites, particularly the Web aggregators, seem to be moving toward the ephemeral. Yet others, including some TV sites, may move the other way, toward collecting deeper reports than they offer now. And the arrival of citizens into the mix seems to push further toward more significant or longer-term issues. The blogosphere may have been the platform least focused on the immediate of any that we monitored.

- While the news is always on, there is not a constant flow of new events. The level of repetition in the 24-hour news cycle is one of the most striking features one finds in examining a day of news. Google News, for instance, offers consumers access to some 14,000 stories from its front page, yet on this day they were actually accounts of the same 24 news events. On cable, just half of the stories monitored across the 12 hours were new. The concept of news cycle is not really obsolete, and the notion of news 24-7 is something of an exaggeration.

To study a day in the life in the media, we picked a universe to be representative of a broad swath of what Americans can choose from. It included three national newspapers, the three primary cable news channels, the three major commercial broadcast networks, PBS, seven news Web sites, seven prominent blogs, and a wide cross-section of TV, radio, newspapers, and ethnic and alternative media in three American cities, Houston, Milwaukee, and Bend, Ore. The result was a study that included 2,125 stories in 57 outlets and 48 hours of programming on radio and television, all offered in a single day, May 11, 2005—plus 112 different blog postings. (Newspapers were coded for the following morning, May 12. For the full list of outlets, please see the methodology.)

To what extent did any of what we saw reflect more than this one day? The results, it turns out—about topics covered, sourcing, and more, in each medium—closely mirror what we have found in these media and others for the last two years, when we took randomly constructed months of news for each, analyzed them by topic and broke down the reporting.

THE MEDIA CULTURE: A LOOSE TYPOLOGY

If different media offer distinctly different news agendas, what did we find about each in our study of May 11?

Online: "The Internet," we found, describes a technology, not a style of media or a set of values or even a journalistic approach. The seven news Web sites we monitored varied widely—from Google's emphasis on speed and bulk to Yahoo's focus on navigability to a local TV news station's site, largely a portal for advertising copy. Many of the most popular sites also remain largely a stepchild of print and wire-service content, especially the so-called Internet-only sites that produce no copy of their own. As a result, while the Internet has added more outlets from which to choose, it has not, our study suggests, added new topics to the agenda.

Ultimately, it still seems unclear what online news will come to represent. Will it be constant updating, focusing on being fast and first? Or more depth, as sites are freed from the confines of space and time? Will online journalism come to mean multi-media convergence, including downloading sound and pictures to PDAs and phones? Or a worrisome intermingling of advertising and editorial? Or will online journalism move toward more citizen voices, more communication with the audience, and more opinion? In the seven sites studied we found all of the above, but none of it all in one place. Two of the most innovative sites we encountered, interestingly, were from old media, a TV network (CBS) and a mid-sized metropolitan newspaper (the *Milwaukee Journal Sentinel*).

Blogs: If the media culture needs navigators, by day's end the seven popular blogs we studied would offer that—to an extent. As the hours went by, the bloggers sifted through the content of the mainstream media and noted what they deemed important, curious, absent, interesting or objectionable. But contrary to the charge that the blogosphere is purely parasitic, we also found new topics here, and new angles on old ones. Indeed, the blogs were generally less concerned than many traditional journalists with the latest breaking news, and more focused on long-term issues. Yet there was little here that a journalist would call reporting or even sourcing. Only 1% of the posts this day involved a blogger doing an interview, and only another 5% involved some other kind of original research, such as examining documents. There is no summary of the news to be had here. The blogs ultimately are idiosyncratic. It is not citizen journalism in any traditional sense, but something closer to a stylized citizen media forum, often with an insider's tone and its own nomenclature.

Cable News: Up close, the striking thing about much of cable news, the first 24-hour medium, is a fixation with whatever is happening at the moment. The result is a good deal of repetition and a good deal that is ephemeral. The reporting, perhaps because of the time to fill rather than despite it, was shallowest by our indicators of any national media studied.

To a degree that we do not find on network TV, the three main cable news channels have also grown distinct from each other. Fox has built its appeal around trying to help its viewers put the news in some order—a conservative order—even if the production values are sometimes ragged. CNN is far more earnest, and tied to the immediate, and seems less sure what the difference is between its different programs. MSNBC, for its part, seems a different channel virtually from program to program—sometimes an extension of NBC News, sometimes something quite alien from its broadcast cousin. If there is a common thread between Don Imus in the morning, Chris Matthews in the evening and Keith Olbermann at night, it might be an effort at being ironic and glib.

Network: The contrast between the network nightly and morning news is so striking that the term network TV news almost seems a misnomer. It makes more sense to talk nightly news versus morning. The three evening newscasts were virtually identical to each other and very different from their network siblings in the morning.

A close look also suggests just how disadvantaged the traditional 30-minute evening newscasts are today. They are still trying to cover traditional hard news, but they are constrained by airing only once a day, by a newshole that is really 18 minutes, and by limited staff, which seems even more apparent when you look closely. People who want a quick, one-shot fill on the major national and international events of the day can still find that here, but within set viewing times and brevity of a 30 minute program.

In the mornings, the luxury of an hour time slot makes a difference, but the news agenda is lighter and focused on emotion. Morning News and Features would probably be a more fitting title. Much, too, depends on the ability of two or three anchors to be experts in everything, prepared for everything, and charming all at the same time.

Newspapers: If ink on paper has an advantage, the day would suggest it is in the number of boots on the ground. This is the medium that is covering the most topics, has the deepest sourcing, explores the most angles in stories, and for now is supplying most of the content for the Internet. A reader also discovers probably the closest thing to a medium still trying to provide all the news a consumer might want, though perhaps in language and sourcing tilted toward elites. Looming, as readers inevitably shift to acquiring their news online, is the question of what happens to the more complete reporting that additional time affords. And how many boots will be left on the ground if the print editions that pay the bills continue to shrink.

Local TV: Local TV, at least in the three cities studied, focused on what news managers apparently thought people could use, traffic and weather, and what they were worried about, accidents and crime. Take out traffic, weather and sports, indeed, and half of all the newshole—and an even greater percentage of lead stories—was devoted to crime and accidents. But the bulk of what made up local news in print—issues like government, taxes, infrastructure and civic institutions—was relegated here to brief "tell" stories in the middle of the newscast. In style and format, the stations were strikingly similar, even across cities. The stories here were just the facts. There was little opinion, our statistical breakdown shows. But on average local TV news stories had the shallowest sourcing and explored the fewest angles of events covered of any medium studied except local radio.

Radio: Contrary to the notion that radio news is all syndicated national material, we found local radio news today to be very local—but also limited in scope. What listeners get is headlines read from wires, adapted from the newspaper, or provided by national networks. The stories are brief—almost always less than a minute and often less than 30 seconds. What depth of coverage we found came largely from talk show hosts offering opinions on issues or taking call-ins from listeners. But we found little in the way of reporters in the field, or what most journalists would consider reporting. Over all, just 14% of stories would involve field reports, and many were from syndicated network feeds. And the eight stations in three cities monitored this day are strikingly alike, in format and style.

CHRONOLOGY OF THE DAY: THE EARLY NEWS—WAKING UP TO HEADLINES

The news day begins awfully early. By 5 a.m., local radio has already entered its magic period, drive time. Those who tune in will get much the same thing in every city—except where the talk shows have already begun—a troika of headlines, traffic and weather. On KTRH in Houston, it's news of a state tax bill, a metro rail crash, threats at a local school, a Vioxx trial. And contrary to the idea that radio is now all national syndication, half of all headlines this day are local. But anyone looking for in-depth reporting here won't find much of it, in early drive time or later.

Local TV news is already on, too, and those who tune in are greeted this day with sirens, overnight homicides, weather maps and traffic cams. The few pieces with reporters are mostly about crimes or accidents—that metro rail crash in Houston, a double homicide in Milwaukee. The rest of the news is handled by anchors reading quick "tell" stories, just as on radio. What distinguishes local TV is that the weather and traffic coverage is the most detailed on any media studied.

Once to the front door, people who pick up the morning paper find a far broader scope of the news—this medium is still trying to offer the full menu—from complete sports to the full range of both national and local news. Even the smaller paper in Bend, Ore., features *New York Times* and *Washington Post* foreign coverage. Even if one has already listened to local radio, or caught the 15-minute news cycle on local TV, the stories here are more complete versions of the headlines they would have heard elsewhere. The *New York Times* and *L.A. Times* are giving big play to the default by United Airlines on its pension plans. In Houston, late night tax bill maneuvering by the state legislature is major news. Milwaukee, it's election fraud and bumbling efforts by Marquette University to change the name of its sports teams.

And those who wander to a computer this early find basically the morning newspapers and wire services. Google's lead story is about a "grenade found near Bush's speech site," from the English-language service of the Chinese news agency Xinhua. In most American papers the story is just a few paragraphs inside. Yahoo! is leading with the murder case in Zion, Ill., and the grenade near Bush. There is only minimal updating with overnight news—riots in Afghanistan and violence in Iraq—but they're on the *New York Times* Web site as well.

7 A.M. : THE NETWORK AND CABLE MORNING

At 7 a.m., TV viewers get a major change in their news day when broadcast television shifts from local programming to network.

"Was the president's life in danger?" Katie Couric asks as she opens NBC's "Today," television news's longest-running weekday program. "The Secret Service investigates a grenade scare overseas." The news agenda is decidedly different from what one was hearing on local news—and softer than what one gets online or in print. There is more emphasis on celebrity, lifestyle and consumer risk, and the crime, since it's not local, tends to bend toward the lurid. The top stories in the first hour are whether the president's life was in danger from that grenade (apparently it wasn't), the grisly murder in Illinois (a story that would vanish in a couple of days), a woman killed in an amusement park accident (not covered elsewhere), a new ATM scam, a mistaken mastectomy, a new Rolling Stone tour, Nancy Reagan and interviews with the winners of CBS's "Amazing Race."

The tone is more informal than on local TV, too (rather than anchor desk, there are love seats and coffee mugs) and more emotional (words like "horrific" and "stunning" are used to set up stories and to conclude them).

For those who prefer cable news, the Fox and CNN morning shows are chatty and informal, too, but without the focus on emotion or lighter fare and with more politics. (CNN covers the grenade story and the murder, but also violence in Iraq and global warming. Fox airs a piece on a move in Congress for ID tags for immigrants and reports questions about homeland security alerts from that morning's *USA Today*). To connect with viewers, apparently, the cable hosts this day offer their political opinions—conservative on Fox, liberal on CNN. "The Bush team criticized John Kerry for suggesting the war would cost $200 billion," the CNN correspondent Andy Serwer says in a dig at the administration. "And, in fact, it's costing $200 billion to date." Adds the anchor Soledad O'Brien: "You're right, and it will probably cost more."

Those who dip into the blogosphere will find it is also already humming by 7 a.m.—the first posts came in as early as 1:18 a.m. EST (Eschaton), but the agenda here is more professorial and much more targeted than in the dreaded MSM. At Talking Points Memo, Josh Marshall this morning is worried about the current Senate debate on the filibuster rule. Eschaton is worrying about falling U.S. wages and Crooks and Liars is writing about a Baptist preacher ousted for political comments made to his congregation.

9 A.M. TO MIDDAY: THE WAITING GAME

By nine a.m., people are getting to work or settling into a quiet house and can go online or to cable news for the latest headlines. But there aren't all that many new things to report. The North Korea and Iraq stories available at 7 a.m. have now been fleshed out with video and background links, especially on CBS News and CNN. (Those stories, incidentally, will carry through to the next day's papers.)

The cable channels, meanwhile, are eagerly awaiting those top news stories they promised they would follow. The problem is there isn't anything to report yet. Macaulay Culkin is expected to testify at Michael Jackson's trial, but all we see are shots of the courthouse door he will walk through. The prosecutor in the Illinois murder is supposed to hold a press conference but it is delayed, and again and again we see shots of the mike stand where he is expected to speak.

NOON: FIFTEEN MINUTES OF BREAKING NEWS

Suddenly, at noon, news breaks out. The White House is being evacuated. So, moments later, are the Capitol and Supreme Court. For those getting online news alerts, or watching TV, the moment is scary. On cable, there are pictures of people running. "This is not a drill," a policeman is heard yelling. A plane, we hear, has violated D.C. airspace.

In 15 minutes, it's over. The plane was a single-engine Cessna gone off course that failed to respond to radio warnings. Finally, about a mile from the White House, the plane reacted to visual contact from Air Force jets. The whole business was a false alarm.

Yet CNN viewers would hear of virtually nothing else the rest of the day. For the next six hours, the news channel would veer from the plane scare just three times, once to brief on Culkin's testimony in the Jackson trial, once for a quick update on Congress for "Inside Politics," and briefly during the second half of Lou Dobbs's business and economics show.

People going online after lunch, when Internet news sites get a surge in traffic around 1 p.m., would find the plane story dominating there, too, at least for a while. NYTimes.com would post at 3:20 p.m., with a more complete account. CNN.com would have updated twice. And Google, for some reason, would be featuring the Canadian Broadcasting Corporation's account. On CBSNews.com the Jackson trial would already have supplanted the plane scare as the lead.

On local news as the afternoon moves on, what captivated the breathless narrators on CNN and the editors of national Web sites would be only a passing headline.

Listeners to local radio in Houston hear a few seconds on the incident before turning back to talk about divorce on KTRH. In Milwaukee, the subject quickly returns to Marquette's nickname on WTMJ, and on WHBL in Sheboygan, Wis., to a beef between the mayor and police officers. As the day moves into drive time, traffic and weather become more important again. The same is true on local TV by mid-afternoon. At 5 p.m., the focus is on local news, and more traffic and weather. The stations in Houston are still leading with the aftermath of that traffic fatality the night before, with repeats of much of the video seen last night and early this morning. In Milwaukee, the story is Marquette's nickname and a police union election.

And for denizens of the blogosphere, the transitory nature of the plane scare made it even less significant a topic. Here, the subjects ranged instead from a blogger convention in Nashville (Instapundit) to a terror alert on a British Airways flight (Little Green Footballs) to a headline in Google News about a Holocaust memorial (Powerline). The criteria of significance on the blogs, it seems, are not so tied to immediacy.

NETWORK NEWS AND THE DINNER HOUR: THE EVENING ROUNDUPS

There was a time, a generation ago, when the news cycle was winding down by 6:30. It ended, except for late local news, after the network nightly newscasts carried their accounts of national and international events. The three news divisions had a monopoly over the video of these stories. Americans then waited until the morning newspapers if they wanted more details. That long ago ceased being the case, and the changeover accelerated in the last five years with the evolution of the Internet.

But 27 million Americans still tune in to see what the news operations of ABC, CBS and NBC say happened for the day, and on this night at least, it is the story that has dominated cable and the Internet. The D.C. plane scare is the lead story on all three programs, making up roughly the first five to six minutes. The networks try to offer something more than their new rivals—minute-by-minute chronologies and discussions about how the air security system works. But the reports, beyond the basic facts of the event, have a hasty and speculative quality. The authorities won't say how the system works. Some think the evacuation was a gross overreaction. Others say the system works beautifully. It also mattered little this day which program one watched. The first 12 minutes of each covered the same stories—after the plane scare, violence in Iraq, then a follow on the United Airlines pensions. The stories that were major fare on cable and the network morning shows that day—the grenade story, the Zion murder and Michael Jackson—are largely skipped.

On PBS, the NewsHour with Jim Lehrer offers viewers an altogether different news agenda of this day than they can find virtually anywhere else on television. After brief accounts in its news summary of the plane scare and violence in Iraq, the newscast focuses on the pension story, melting in the Arctic circle, and a background discussion on the fights in the Senate over judicial nominations that have intensified the political polarization in Washington. The segments are long, nine to 12 minutes, and the interviews often involve three experts, not one. The contrast is such that one wonders whether public broadcasting will try to expand into other parts of the day, as NPR has done on radio.

A NIGHT IN CABLE NEWS: ATTITUDE, OPINION, AND IRONY

The national news day would once have ended now, but for cable viewers, in many ways, the heat is just turning on. Even more so than during the day, at night the cable news channels are quite varied as they counter-program off each other to maximize audience, one going with talk, another with news, another business, and then an hour later reshuffling the deck.

At 6:00 p.m., Fox's most politics- and policy-focused program, "Special Report with Brit Hume," gives its audience one of the more complete studies of the plane scare seen on TV this day. On MSNBC, the Washington "hardball" insider Chris Matthews (on the network's top-rated show) tells viewers he loved a new book by a fellow GE employee, Tim Russert (it left him "crying") and about a tribute that night to Nancy Reagan. CNN's Lou Dobbs's gives viewers more plane scare, plus a little on North Korean nuclear claims, riots in Afghanistan and Iraq car bombings.

There is no clear time slot for a signature evening newscast on cable, nor are there programs that really resemble them. On Fox, the evening news summary arguably is split between Hume and, an hour later, "The Fox Report with Shepard Smith." On MSNBC, the closest thing viewers get is "Countdown with Keith Olbermann," where the subject is as much Olbermann's take on the news as the news itself. He is telling viewers, among other things, about the plane scare (the coverage was overblown), a football player caught with a device called a Wizzonater (Olbermann raises his generous eyebrows over the name) which could help conceal drug use, and a Michael Jackson "Puppet Theater" he is auctioning off on eBay.

The audience for CNN's evening summary newscast, meanwhile, "NewsNight with Aaron Brown" (since replaced by "Anderson Cooper 360") learns all about the plane scare from five different angles—and there is no irony, thank you.

At some point during the evening viewers can get at least one talk show on each news channel. On Fox the No. 1 rated "O'Reilly Factor" is focused on an editorial in the *Westchester County Journal News* which, Bill O'Reilly says, is "true and dumb," on the Macaulay Culkin testimony—"why should I care?"—and on the "continuing meltdown of the American criminal justice system." On CNN, top-rated Larry King offers no opinions as he talks with Secretary of State Condoleezza Rice.

By 9 p.m., users will find that online news Web sites have slowed down, even though this is prime time for overall traffic. CBSNews.com is still leading with that Jackson story. The *New York Times* has an updated account of the plane scare posted at 7 p.m. Click 2 Houston, the Web site of the NBC affiliate in town, where "Local News Comes First," is still on that pickup truck that crashed into a metro rail train the night before. And Google is leading with the Reuters account for the next morning's papers of the plane scare, followed, oddly, by a 7-hour-old account of that grenade incident from the Chinese news agency. The next day's papers have not posted. That will come sometime closer to midnight.

In the blogosphere, some have signed off by 8 p.m. The others are offering opinions on one of their brethren's experiences on the Michael Medved talk radio show (Eschaton), a Senate report on Iraqi oil allocations (Power Line), and a blogger getting "overly exercised" about Bush's recent comments about Yalta (Instapundit).

The news cycle won't end, but people eventually do go to sleep. Their news cycle ends. For some, it will come after the local news.

JON STEWART, THE LAST WORD

For others, it may come with a different accounting of the day from Jon Stewart on the "Daily Show." Stewart, whose program airs on Comedy Central but is a source of news for many of its viewers, opened his show, like the network newscasts, with the Cessna that flew into restricted D.C. air space. But rather than focusing on whether policy makers did or didn't do the right thing, or how big a story this was or wasn't, the "Daily Show" focused on something viewers might have noticed. "The important thing is in the three-and-half years since 9-11 we have made tremendous progress in dealing with these situations," Stewart says. "A new strategy has been implemented. It worked to perfection today. It's called (pause) run for your lives."

The show also turns its attention to North Korea and its weapons program, another major story in the media culture this day, and his target here is just how fuzzy the official estimates seemed to be about how many weapons North Korea might be able to make. "Ahhh, half-dozenish, 10 million casualties give or take, you know." There is rant from Comedian Lewis Black, a "This Week in God Segment" and an installment of "Great Moments in Punditry as Read by Children."

After a day in which many Americans may have been exposed to images, bits of news, earnest commentators, alarmist codewords, pompous newsmakers and maybe pompous news providers, a sense of absurdity can come to mind. The "Daily Show" articulates that.

CONCLUSION

In the end, one does draw some conclusions about the different media—what they offer and what they do not. None excel at everything. And there are few, if any, news consumers who rely on only one of these outlets anymore.

The Day in the Life of the News offers two warnings, as well. Consuming the news continuously does not mean being better informed. There is too much repetition, and too much confusion. The most efficient diet means finding the right mix depending on the time of the day, the nature of the news that day, and more. The wrong mix may prove to be a waste of time, the one thing consumers can never get back.

FOOTNOTES

1. This story count includes every channel that aired a segment about the incident. Brief anchor reads of a headline about the incident are excluded.

Our Opinion*

Accuracy the Victim of 24-hour News Cycle

Times Record News (Wichita Falls, Tex.), November 9, 2009

At first, we heard that seven people had been killed and 20 wounded in a pair of shootings at Fort Hood Army base in Texas.

We knew, unfortunately, from reporting on massive shootings such as those at Columbine and Virginia Tech University, the death toll would sadly rise, and rise quickly.

The shooting, first reported at about 2 p.m., Thursday became the wall-to-wall coverage on 24-7 news outlets scrambling to fill the white space between initial reports and confirmations.

At TimesRecordNews.com, we waited for confirmation from The Associated Press, posting a breaking news alert within the hour.

Conflicting information filtered out of the tragedy all afternoon.

A pair of shootings, one at a medical processing center, another at a theater.

Three gunmen wearing fatigues.

Fatigues, at the largest base in the free world—that's a safe guess.

Battle stress over repeated deployments.

The suspect is dead.

The heroic female police officer who gunned down the suspect also was killed.

Record-high suicide rates and other signs of stress could be contributing factors.

A suspect with an Arabic-sounding name.

A suspect who converted after 9-11.

TV anchors pondering when the suspect may have changed his name, assuming that because his name is Arabic and we're at war in two Muslim countries, he must be a terrorist.

Twitter becomes the "reliable" source of eyewitness reporting, even though we have no idea from where the tweets are coming.

Wait, not so fast.

Not three shooters, just one.

Not a Muslim convert, but an American-born Muslim who had never changed his name.

Not dead. Seven hours later, we learn the suspect hadn't died after all but was, in fact, in stable condition. How could that have gotten so twisted?

Not suffering from combat fatigue, since the suspect had never deployed to the Middle East.

Now, several news cycles after the tragedy unfolded, we know a lot more. And we knew we would. But in today's race to be first and the struggle to fill the white space, news outlets throw whatever they hear out there, and worry about picking up the refuted pieces later.

It's as if 24-hour news doesn't realize that what they've said, even if it's refuted, is out there, forever. Every Twitter remains. Every update stays on the Web.

Only extreme news junkies, with little else to do, watch 24-7 and see the recants. Most of us are just passing through the living room, picking up tidbits that could be, down the road, completely debunked.

This is what we've grown accustomed to, though, buckshot reporting, filler, something to keep us hooked.

Journalism's motto used to be: "Be first but be right."

One out of two isn't enough.

Cable News Divides to Conquer[*]

Partisan Voices on Rise in Election Cycle

By Cynthia Littleton and Michael Learmonth
Variety, August 20–26, 2007

It was MSNBC's programming triumph of the summer: a pep rally for 15,000 liberals and seven Democratic presidential hopefuls in Chicago's Soldier Field, emceed by the cabler's marquee anchor, Keith Olbermann.

Not that Olbermann didn't ask tough questions during the AFL-CIO-sponsored Democratic Presidential Forum, which MSNBC carried live on Aug. 7. But everything about the event—the setting, the audience of union members and their families, the star moderator and the tenor of the candidates' campaign shoutin' —seemed tailor-made to appeal to the average reader of the Huffington Post.

"For 15 years, I've stood up against the right-wing machine and I've come out stronger," Hillary Clinton declared to one of the loudest applause outbursts of the 90-minute event. "If you want a winner who knows how to take them on, I'm your girl!"

The image of a football stadium full of (mostly) Democrats cheering and pumping their fists offers a stark illustration of the increasingly partisan tilt to much of cable television's political news coverage. In the old days, TV news, like most mainstream journalism orgs, took pride in maintaining a non-partisan stance. Now, that attitude seems antiquated amid competitive pressures and a growing sentiment among the public that most media coverage of politics is heavily biased anyway.

The rise of strident partisan voices on all-news cablers is a longtime trend that has gone into overdrive during this elongated presidential election cycle. The polarization of the TV dial is being driven by a confluence of forces within the television industry and the body politic.

Perhaps the most significant cause has been the public's steady disengagement from politics and elections, as evidenced by the long-term decline in voter turnout for presidential elections from a peak of nearly 65% of the voting-age population in 1960 to less than 50% in 1996 (though turnout did spike, to 55% in 2004). That turnoff of politics and politicians means the most likely viewers for political news coverage are political junkies who come to the set with strong opinions in place.

"There are fewer and fewer people reading a daily newspaper, and fewer and fewer people tuning in to the nightly network news. That diminishes the (media's) ability to have a nonpartisan conversation about politics that engages everyone," says Tom Hollihan, a professor of media and politics at USC's Annenberg School for Communication. "What you have now is (all-news) networks trying to reach those people who are most interested in politics. Those are people who tend to be intensely partisan and have a take-no-prisoners attitude to politics."

Moreover, opinion-oriented talk shows that are largely done in-studio are a lot cheaper to produce than sending a crew of reporters and producers on the campaign trail for reporting.

"That's a business decision for networks," Hollihan says.

The TV biz has undergone a nicheification process with the growth of cable and satellite distribs. More recently, the explosion of news and information sources on the Internet and the concept of a national political conversation has given way to the "echo chamber" effect, in which the politically engaged "are drawn to those (media) sources that tell you what you want to believe," Hollihan says.

From its birth in 1996, Fox News Channel has tubthumped itself as a "fair and balanced" antidote to the long-held perception of a liberal bias in TV news, specifically at CNN. In the past year, MSNBC has embraced the left, at least for one hour a night, with its irreverent but clearly liberal-leaning 8 p.m. news roundup program "Countdown With Keith Olbermann."

"Countdown" has been on MSNBC since April 2003, but its viewership has spiked during the past year, ever since its host began offering a semi-regular, often-fiery commentary segment in which he has inveighed against the GOP's agenda and called for the resignations of President Bush and Vice President Cheney.

For the month of July, viewership of "Countdown" rose 88% year-to-year to a nightly average of 721,000 viewers, still well behind Fox News' 8 p.m. anchor "The O'Reilly Factor," which averaged 2 million viewers.

MSNBC's Aug. 7 debate, meanwhile, drew 939,000 viewers in its live telecast— nearly double the channel's primetime average in July of 529,000 viewers but low by the standards of other cable news debates—and a midnight ET repeat brought in another 433,000 viewers.

"You're not going to survive in cable doing a straight news-of-record broadcast," says Phil Griffin, senior veep of NBC News and the exec in charge at MSN-BC. "You've got to give (more) information and analysis. . . . By 8 at night, most people who tune in have a basic understanding of the news of the day."

Olbermann's liberal stance contrasts to most other big personalities in cable news, including MSNBC's own Joe Scarborough and Chris Matthews, and Glenn Beck on CNN's Headline News offshoot. MSNBC's opportunistic move to counterprogram the prevailing winds with an anchor like Olbermann was only a matter of time, observers say.

"Look at how the Bush presidency has motivated liberals to become really engaged again," USC's Hollihan says. "It's only a surprise that it took a network so long to figure out that there was this audience out there."

In some ways the trend in cable seems to be a throwback to a few generations ago, when competing daily newspapers would align themselves as staunchly pro-Republican or pro-Democrat. And it mirrors the well-documented trend of conservative voices taking root on the influential platform of talkradio during the past 20-odd years.

The starkest example of the current electronic partisan divide has been the major Democratic candidates' decision to pull out of a debate that was to have been hosted this month by Fox News. The pullout was in protest over a public quip by Fox News chairman Roger Ailes that was interpreted by some as equating Democratic candidate Barack Obama with Osama bin Laden. (CNN and MSNBC have hosted events this year with candidates from both major parties; MSNBC sent "Hardball" anchor Chris Matthews to moderate its GOP event in May.)

The Dems' boycott of the Fox News debate has drawn a fair amount of criticism, even from liberals. "If you can't stand up to (Fox News') Chris Wallace, can you stand up to terrorists? Or the Republican Party?" Bill Maher quipped on CNN's "Larry King Live."

But even if it strikes some as a bit precious, the Dems' stance is reflective of the general public's sentiment toward the media, according to a survey released this month by the Pew Research Center for the People and the Press. The telephone survey of 1,503 adults conducted late last month found that 55% of respondents believe the news media (broadly categorized as local and network TV and newspapers) are politically biased, up from 45% in 1985, while 36% of respondents believe that news organizations "hurt democracy," up from 23% in 1985.

But Republicans tend to be more critical of the news media than Democrats, the survey found. Some 70% of respondents who identified themselves as Republicans said they felt the news media was politically biased in its reporting, compared with 39% of Democrats. (The perception gap between the two sides was much smaller when the survey was first conducted in 1985, when 49% of GOPers smelled bias, compared with 43% of Dems.) Some 63% of Republicans surveyed said they felt stories and reports by the news media are "often inaccurate," compared with 43% of Democratic respondents.

One of the biggest drawbacks of the news media's decline in credibility and the increase in partisan chatter on the airwaves is the impact it has had on public policy debates—especially on complex pieces of business like the recent immigration reform bill that flamed out amid much finger-pointing and cries of "sellout" aimed at pols in both parties who sought a compromise on the thorniest issues in the bill.

The chorus of complaints from those who hew to a strict party line can drown out more reasoned efforts to examine the nuances of what's really at stake in big public policy issues like Social Security reform or an overhaul of Medicare.

"Opinions (in the news media) can be helpful," says Al Tompkins of the Florida-based journo think tank Poynter Institute, "but only if the people giving the opinions know what they're talking about."

As USC's Hollihan observes: "In a world where fewer people are paying attention to big public policy issues, (politicos) are really under pressure to please those who are paying close attention."

Bibliography

Books

Allan, Stuart, and Einar Thorsen. *Citizen Journalism: Global Perspectives*. New York: Peter Lang Publishing, 2009.

Alterman, Eric. *What Liberal Media? The Truth About Bias and the News*. New York: Basic Books, 2003.

Beckett, Charlie. *Supermedia: Saving Journalism So It Can Save the World*. Malden, Mass.: Wiley-Blackwell, 2008.

Downie, Leonard Jr., and Robert J. Kaiser. *The News About the News: American Journalism in Peril*. New York: Vintage, 2003.

Fenton, Tom. *Bad News: The Decline of Reporting, the Business of News, and the Danger to Us All*. New York: William Morrow: 2005.

Gant, Scott E. *We're All Journalists Now: The Transformation of the Press and Reshaping of the Law in the Internet Age*. New York: Free Press, 2007.

Gillmor, Dan. *We the Media: Grassroots Journalism by the People, for the People*. Sebastopol, Calif.: O'Reilly Media, 2004.

Goldberg, Bernard. *Bias: A CBS Insider Exposes How the Media Distort the News*. Washington, D.C.: Regnery Publishing, Inc., 2001.

Henderson, Harry. *Power of the News Media*. New York: Facts on File, 2004.

Henry, Neil. *American Carnival: Journalism under Siege in an Age of New Media*. Berkeley and Los Angeles: University of California Press, 2007.

Jones, Alex S. *Losing the News: The Future of the News that Feeds Democracy*. New York: Oxford University Press, USA, 2009.

Kennedy, George, and Daryl Moen, eds. *What Good Is Journalism? How Reporters and Editors Are Saving America's Way of Life*. Columbia, Mo.: University of Missouri Press, 2007.

Madigan, Charles M., ed. *-30-: The Collapse of the Great American Newspaper*. Chicago: Ivan R. Dee, 2007.

McChesney, Robert W., and John Nichols. *The Death and Life of American Journalism: The Media Revolution that Will Begin the World Again*. New York: Nation Books, 2010

Merritt, Davis. *Knightfall: Knight-Ridder and How the Erosion of Newspaper Journalism Is Putting Democracy at Risk*. New York: AMACOM, 2005.

Meyer, Philip. *The Vanishing Newspaper: Saving Journalism in the Information Age*, Second Edition. Columbia, Mo.: University of Missouri Press, 2009.

Rosenberg, Howard, and Charles S. Feldman. *No Time to Think: The Menace of Media Speed and the 24-Hour News Cycle*. New York: Continuum, 2008.

Wasik, Bill. *And Then There's This: How Stories Live and Die in Viral Culture*. New York: Viking Press, 2009.

Web Sites

Readers seeking additional information on the news and its future may wish to consult the following Web sites, all of which were operational as of this writing.

American Journalism Review (AJR)

www.ajr.org

A national magazine published six times per year, *American Journalism Review* provides coverage of all facets of the news industry. Its Web site gives users access to feature articles, back issues, links to a variety of other media- and journalism-related sites, and a host of additional content.

Columbia Journalism Review (CJR)

www.cjr.org

The mission of Columbia Journalism Review (CJR) "is to encourage and stimulate excellence in journalism in the service of a free society." The organization was founded in 1961 and is affiliated with Columbia University's Graduate School of Journalism. The CJR's multimedia Web site allows visitors to read material from CJR magazine, which is published six times a year, and access other on-line content, including blogs and various CJR projects.

CyberJournalist.net

www.cyberjournalist.net

Launched in 2000, this Web site explores how the Internet and other technological innovations are changing the media and journalism. Most of the original content on CyberJournalist.net is produced by the site's founder, Jonathan Dube, an award-winning media professional. The site offers particularly strong coverage of such issues as "Innovation," "Future of Media," and "Social Media."

FAIR: Fairness & Accuracy in Reporting

www.fair.org

Founded in 1986, FAIR is a national media monitoring group that seeks to uncover examples of bias and censorship. Visitors to the Web site can view the latest organization news, including the FAIR blog, and access articles from Extra!, a monthly magazine featuring media criticism.

Knight Digital Media Center

www.knightdigitalmediacenter.org

A partnership between the University of Southern California (USC)'s Annenberg School for Communication and the University of California at Berkeley's Graduate School of Journalism, the Knight Digital Media Center "is dedicated to helping good journalists and good journalism succeed in the 21st century by providing training for New Media at all levels," according to its Web site. Among the on-line resources available to users are access to awards lists, tutorials, such blogs as OJR: Online Journalism Review, and other material.

New Media Institute (NMI)

www.newmedia.org

The New Media Institute (NMI) is a research organization dedicated to improving "public understanding of issues surrounding the Internet and other forms [of] new media communications," according to its Web site. Visitors have access to "New Media News," "Webinars," an "Internet Law Library," and other multimedia content.

Project for Excellence in Journalism (PEJ)

www.journalism.org

Affiliated with the Pew Research Center, the nonpartisan Project for Excellence in Journalism (PEJ) "is dedicated to trying to understand the information revolution." By gathering and examining data, the Project seeks to study the performance of the news media. Visitors to the PEJ's Web site can view both the raw statistics compiled by the Project as well as its analysis.

Society of Professional Journalists (SPJ)

www.spj.org

Since 1909, this organization has been "dedicated to encouraging the free practice of journalism and stimulating high standards of ethical behavior." The Society is composed of almost 10,000 professional journalists. Its Web site offers news on the organization's various projects as well as links to its journal, *Quill*, and other material.

Additional Periodical Articles with Abstracts

More information about the news and its future can be found in the following articles. Readers interested in additional articles may consult the *Readers' Guide to Periodical Literature* and other H.W. Wilson publications.

Notice What You Notice. Beth Macy. *American Journalism Review* v. 30 pp46–51 August/ September 2008.

Macy, who is the families beat reporter at the *Roanake Times*, describes her efforts to find interesting topics to write about in her columns and outlines the lessons she has learned from other columnists about how to find inspiration. She discusses the importance of writing about the things that attract her attention as she goes about her business, the use of maintaining an idea-gathering system by filing interesting clippings for possible column fodder, the need for reporters to see what is going on first-hand instead of staying in the newsroom and gathering stories over the phone, and the need to write stories that move, inspire, and delight readers.

A False Rivalry: Between Newspapers and New-Media Journalism. Barb Palser. *American Journalism Review* v. 28 p62 June/July 2006.

The misunderstanding between traditional and new-media journalists is clouding conversations about the future of news and creating unnecessary acrimony, Palser reports. He claims that blaming on-line publishing for some of the changes happening in print newsrooms and establishing a "print versus Internet" rivalry is false and damaging. There is no reason, Palser writes, to believe that on-line news is essentially cheap and shallow, and he adds that focusing the conversation on newspapers gives other journalists a false sense of detachment, the language of rivalry allowing print journalists to regard the Internet as something alien and intimidating. Those concerned about the future of newspapers might garner greater support, Palser maintains, if they spoke inclusively about the types of journalism they wish to safeguard, and they should concede that other journalists might be their best allies in protecting those principles.

Getting Over Ourselves: Newspapers Finding Ways to Market Themselves in New Media. Rem Rieder. *American Journalism Review* v. 28 p6 June/July 2006.

The writer reflects on the irrevocable change that has happened to the media landscape due to the combination of the Internet and Wall Street profit pressures and argues that journalists simply have to accept it.

Appeal to Authority. James Taranto. *The American Spectator* v. 42 pp56–57 October 2009.

In the summer of 2009, Dan Rather made a proposal aimed at saving the news business. In a July Aspen Institute speech and an August *Washington Post* op-ed, Rather, styling himself an elder statesman of journalism, endorsed a long-standing leftist critique of the media, namely, that they are controlled by corporations and therefore in the pocket of the government, Taranto reports. Rather said he wants " the president to convene a nonpartisan, blue-ribbon commission to assess the state of the news as an institution and an industry and to make recommendations for improving and stabilizing both." This, Taranto claims, is the flip side of liberal media bias: If Dan Rather gets his presidential commission, it may be the death panel for independent journalism.

Opinionated News. Elizabeth Wasserman. *CQ Weekly* v. 66 p1530 June 9, 2008.

The increasingly blurred line between reporters and partisan commentators is threatening to undermine the credibility of the Washington, D.C., press corps, Wasserman writes. The news that ABC and CBS News veteran Linda Douglass has become a strategist for Barack Obama has riled right-wing interests. The Left was equally perturbed when Karl Rove became a Fox News contributor in February 2008, having stepped down as President George W. Bush's chief political strategist. Indeed, political players at all levels are being hired to fill the seemingly limitless time and space available across media platforms. The question, Wasserman writes, is whether these new pundits are bringing depth and expertise to media coverage or undermining what is left of reportorial objectivity and fueling criticisms of media bias among a disillusioned public.

I've Read the News Today, Oh Boy. Ben Yagoda. *The Chronicle of Higher Education* v. 56 pB24 November 20, 2009.

The writer outlines the results of a thought experiment he conducted in a bid to predict which types of newspaper story will survive the revolution that journalism is currently undergoing. The experiment involved dissecting a recent edition of his local newspaper, *The Philadelphia Inquirer.*

My Facts, Your Facts: America and the Pursuit of Willful Delusion. David Cay Johnston. *Columbia Journalism Review* v. 47 pp59–60 July/August 2008.

True Enough: Learning to Live in a Post-Fact Society, the debut book by former Salon technology columnist Farhad Manjoo, is a challenging and engaging investigation of media bias, Johnston writes. Like beauty, contends Manjoo, bias is in the eye of the beholder, so rather than examining those who report and analyze the news, Manjoo looks at their audience. It is an innovative and revealing approach, Johnston writes. Manjoo insists that "selective perception" is part of the human state, and that in this age of limitless news outlets, it is surprisingly easy for individuals to receive all of their news from places that tell them just what they wish to hear, a sort of segregation of the mind.

The Future of Journalism: Yesterday's Papers. *The Economist* v. 375 pp59–60 April 23, 2005.

News Corporation magnate Rupert Murdoch's speech to the American Society of Newspaper Editors, warning of the potential demise of newspapers, suggested that the stodgy newspaper business has officially woken up to the novel realities of the Internet age, the author of this article writes. Thanks to new media tools provided by the Internet and accelerated by broadband, the author maintains, young people are more likely to find out about current affairs on-line than to buy traditional newspapers. According to Dan Gillmor, the founder of Grassroots Media in San Francisco, this is because they want to be informed but not lectured. Murdoch's comments support the author's claim: The mainstream media belittles or ignores the threat posed by new tools—such as weblogs, or "blogs," which are on-line journal entries; and wikis, collaborative web pages—at their peril.

A Newspaper Can't Love You Back: Impact Journalism and the Prize Culture.
David Simon. *Esquire* v. 149 p110+ March 2008.

The writer, who was a reporter at *The Baltimore Sun* for 13 years, describes his experience of working with the newspaper. Topics discussed include the first public correction that he had to make to an article that he wrote, his love of the journalistic process, the way in which his experience as a successful author helped him to become a better reporter, the challenges presented by new management at the paper, and the changing face of the newspaper business.

The Myth of Pro-Obama Media Bias. John K. Wilson. *Extra!* v. 21 pp8–11 September/October 2008.

One assumption of the 2008 election was that the media loved Barack Obama, but there is little evidence for this, Wilson argues. Conservatives have complained about Obama coverage and corporate media have echoed the GOP's talking points, with the result that the public has started to believe repeated declarations of media bias, Wilson adds. He maintains that the myth of the pro-Obama media is the same as the myth of the liberal press, and it has been created by right-wing pundits who declare repeatedly and vociferously that the media are biased in favor of liberals, by centrist media pundits who concede that the Right might have a point, and by the fact that progressive critics are excluded from the dominant pro-establishment and right-wing talk shows. Although there was substantially more coverage of Obama than any other candidate, that was not unusual, according to data from the Tyndall Report. Moreover, Wilson writes, one of the central themes in the Obama coverage was the accusation of inexperience.

The Negative Effect: News, Politics, and the Public. Thomas E. Patterson. *The Hedgehog Review* v. 10 pp60–68 Summer 2008.

In this article, part of a special issue on the relationship between politics and the media in the United States, Patterson argues that the news media have a bias toward criticism of politicians and the political process, and that this bias is detrimental to political life. The news that people are exposed to has a significant impact on how they view politics, Patterson writes, adding that negative news tends to diminish Americans' respect for their political leaders and institutions. Moreover, he contends, criticism in the news media has generated persistently high levels of public mistrust and dissatisfaction in relation to politics. A significant part of this problem is due to the tendency among journalists to imply that leaders are self-interested to the exclusion of the public good, that their votes can be influenced by moneyed or special interests that do not serve their constituents' ends, and that they are dishonest about what they are trying to achieve and secretly motivated by a desire to stay in power, Patterson writes. The attitude within the media has been negative for too long not to have made an impression, he adds.

I Want to Own That Last Newspaper. Michael Ference. *Hydraulics & Pneumatics* v. 62 p4 April 2009.

The writer discusses the shift from print to online editions of publications. Many publishers are supplying online versions of newspapers and magazines, and subscriptions are increasing. However, it is argued that the online versions often offer only supplemental information to the printed version, that the reader does not own the information in the same way as a purchased newspaper, and that printed editions will continue to be of interest to many readers for the foreseeable future.

The Effects of Media Bias. August John Hoffman and Julie Wallach. *Journal of Applied Social Psychology* v. 37 p616–30 March 2007.

The authors of this study investigated whether bias exists in newspapers that are considered liberal or conservative, and whether this bias influences public opinion of events. Participants were college students (N = 67) who were enrolled in a 4-year university (n = 33) or a community college (n = 34). Participants were shown photographs and short articles relating to a presidential debate between President George W. Bush and Senator John Kerry. Participants completed questionnaires relating to their opinions of the candidates. Results showed statistical significance within groups before and after exposure to the newspaper clippings. Reprinted by permission of the publisher.

The Newspaper Is Dying—Hooray for Democracy. Andrew Potter. *Maclean's* v. 121 p17 April 7, 2008.

The newspaper's demise does not mean the end of democracy, Potter writes, adding that although the newspaper may be in decline, the overall consumption of news is rising, almost entirely due to the many online sources. Some people are increasingly worried that the end of the newspaper is a threat to democracy itself, based on the argument that a newspaper had to bring together a diverse set of voices, presenting each reader with ideas and perspectives that he or she might not otherwise have seen or looked for. Nevertheless, Potter argues that nothing about the way in which people consume media online suggests that they are searching for confirmation of preexisting biases. It actually appears that as people migrate online, Potter reports, it will be to find sources of information that they consider to be unbiased and which give them news unavailable elsewhere.

Order Versus Access: News Search Engines and the Challenge to Traditional Journalistic Roles. Matt Carlson. *Media, Culture & Society* v. 29 pp1014–30 November 2007.

The writer explores how the rise of news search engines that index news stories from across the Web has created tensions between new media forms and traditional journalistic practice. He devotes particular attention to Google News, because of its popularity and its insistence on not using human editors. He observes that on the one hand, traditional news promotes an interpretative order through deliberately structuring the news product to produce a meaningful map of what is significant. On the other hand, he notes, news search engines promote diversity through creating easy access to different viewpoints and multiple versions of a story without legitimating one view over another. He asserts that these conflicting normative articulations of journalism lead to tensions around questions of what journalism does and what it should do.

Refs, Worked (Redux). Eric Alterman. *The Nation* v. 287 p10 December 15, 2008.

Mainstream media (MSM) refs are not simply "doomed to repeat" their historic surrender to right-wing pressure groups but are leading the charge themselves, Alterman writes. Terrified in 2004 by blogger attacks on Dan Rather's carelessly sourced report on George Bush's war avoidance record, network executives attempted, by any means necessary, to appease their accusers, Alterman reports. He adds that a more recent but only slightly less unsettling instance of a similar Stockholm-style syndrome among appointed MSM watchdogs can be found in a few recent columns by *Washington Post* ombudsman Deborah

Howell. Howell contends that the *Post*'s problem is the fact that thousands of conservatives and even some moderates have complained during her three-year-plus term that the paper is too liberal, complaints that she describes as "valid."

A Liberal Supermajority (Finally) Finds Its Voice. Eric Alterman. *The Nation* v. 287 p9 November 17, 2008.

According to the author, Barack Obama has provided an inspirational message for a public keen to espouse the sort of politics that has been condemned and trivialized for the past eight years by mainstream media intent on deflecting the Right's allegations of "liberal bias." Virtually every mainstream media outlet adheres rigidly to right-wing assumptions long since debunked by reality, Alterman writes, with the general election debates providing a clear example. He says that almost all questions related to the financial crisis assumed that the disaster demands a drastic cut in public investment—as if Keynesian economics, instead of Friedmanite economics, were somehow to blame—and almost every foreign policy question assumed that neocon-style threats of the use of force were effective. Many in the MSM have applauded, submitted, or pretended not to notice as America's liberal supermajority has observed the degradation and dishonoring of its nation for the past eight years, Alterman insists.

The End of Times? Eric Alterman. *The Nation* v. 283 p10 November 13, 2006.

The financial foundation of journalism is severely threatened by the Internet, Alterman writes. He maintains that young people do not buy newspapers or watch the evening news, blogs are more fun to read and sometimes more reliable, and traditional revenue streams have been diverted by craigslist, eBay, Yahoo! and Google. Now, newspapers and powerful magazine franchises are shedding large numbers of editorial staff, even though most newspapers, like the network news, are in profit. The fate of the mainstream media is important, Alterman writes, because a substitute is nowhere at hand for the crucial role played by newspapers and the news in keeping society intact. This crisis of U.S. journalism is part of what Alterman calls a larger failure of nerve by virtually all of the country's elites, which did not stand up to the attack on democracy by right-wing ideologues in the Bush administration and elsewhere and have no answer to the societal, moral, and environmental damage caused by an unfettered capitalist machine.

Black and White and Dead All Over: Demise of Newspapers. James DeLong. *National Review* v. 61 pp28–29 April 6, 2009.

Conservatives, exasperated by the dirigiste liberal bent of the mainstream media, should approach print journalism's destruction by concentrating on how to build an energetic, open, and diverse news business from the detritus of the old newspaper business, DeLong argues in this article. Neither locally focused papers nor national news services can run without funds. They have to find a way to finance their products, whether via subscriptions, per-story micropayments, advertising, or all three. That entails control of access and defense against free-riding. As DeLong writes, conservatives have a chance to fashion an odd-couple alliance with *The New York Times* and other journalistic institutions that are griping about how information really wishes to be paid for. People will either have news-collection systems that are based on property and enterprise, DeLong posits, or they will become dependent on foundations and government subsidies for their news, a system that would maintain the liberal bias of the media in an extremely virulent form, protected from market pressure.

MSM, RIP: Crisis in Journalism. *The New Republic* v. 240 p1 March 4, 2009.

Journalism is experiencing what the author of this article deems a legitimacy crisis. Just as the press has been seriously disadvantaged by technology, the writer contends, it has been assaulted by the political culture. The master narratives of the Right and Left now include the same villain—the hypocritical, biased elite media—and their combined complaining has helped to create the anti-media backlash, the author claims, adding that the attack on the credibility of the press destroys its authority in the culture, giving cover to politicians such as members of the Bush administration who would prefer not to deal with reporters. Barack Obama has suggested that he will borrow from Bush and deal with the press as he pleases, but he has not done so of late, the author maintains. Obama now has an opportunity to persuade liberals to ratchet down their hostility toward newspapers and start defending them because a press working toward the ideal of objectivity is often the only way to blunt government or business run amok, the writer concludes.

Come Gather 'Round People. Sara Nelson. *Publishers Weekly* v. 254 p12 May 7, 2007.

According to Nelson, the recent news that several newspapers are making big changes in the way that they cover or, more precisely, will not cover books elicited a predictable response from most in publishing that the move is a disaster. However, Nelson argues, the time has come to stop lamenting and begin coming up with alternatives. Atria's recent declaration that it had made an agreement with a book blogger to guarantee reviews can be seen as a good start, Nelson writes, as are *L.A. Times Book Review* editor David Ulin's plans for the newspaper's Web site. In addition, Nelson suggests, publishers could possibly start to pay for ads to replace the reviews they could not be certain sold books in the first place.

Media Revolution. Seiche Sanders. *Quality Progress* v. 42 p6 July 2009.

The writer discusses the changes in the delivery of news from paper-based media to electronic media and the Internet. The change is partly due to the availability of news online, wrong choices of business model, and increased competition. However, magazines appear to be more robust to the change than newspapers, partly due to the depth of information and insight provided, and to the provision of online resources that complement the magazines.

Election Analysis. Amy Guyer. *The Quill* (Chicago, Ill.) v. 97 pp28–30 April 2009.

In its analyses of the 2008 presidential election, the Pew Research Center examined such issues as the media's dominant focus in the last moths of the campaign and the fairness of the media's campaign coverage. Pew found, among other things, that the public overwhelmingly believed that the media was biased in favor of Barack Obama. Moreover, a Pew poll on October 22, 2008, indicated that while coverage of Obama was favorable, coverage of his Republican opponent John McCain was "heavily unfavorable." It further determined that journalists were primarily concerned not with campaign issues or strategies but with who would win. The media tendency to treat the election campaign as a horse race continues to have ethical implications, Guyer reports.

Canvassing Coverage from Bush to Obama. Scott Leadingham. *The Quill* (Chicago, Ill.) v. 97 pp18–22 April 2009.

In this article, Leadingham compares the media's coverage of President George W. Bush's "nonelection" in 2000 and inauguration in January 2001 with that of President Barack Obama's election in 2008 and his inauguration in January 2009. The media coverage of Bush and Obama invites comparison, Leadingham writes, because neither candidate was seeking reelection and both campaigned for change and bipartisanship. Focusing on the respective coverage in the magazines *Time* and *Newsweek*, as well as the newspapers *The New York Times*, the *Washington Post*, and *The Indianapolis Star*, reveals considerable differences in how the elections were dealt with, Leadingham writes. The author says these differences stem primarily from radical technological changes. If the media was more favorably pre-disposed to Obama than Bush, the bias was more human than political, Leadingham says, adding that journalists covering Obama's election went through the same process that election journalists have always gone through, but on this occasion, they clearly recognized the historical import of the election of the first African-American president and responded accordingly.

Amusing Ourselves to Depth: *The Onion* Contrasted with Other Newspapers. Greg Beato. *Reason* v. 39 pp15–16 November 2007.

Started in 1988 by college student Tim Keck, *The Onion* is one of the newspaper industry's few major success stories of the post-newspaper era, Beato reports. At the time this article was published, 710,000 copies of each weekly edition were being printed, and the paper's circulation had increased by 60 percent over the previous three years. Unlike most newspa-pers, *The Onion* is an extremely honest publication that does not shy away from offending readers or expressing a worldview, Beato writes. He adds that *The Onion*'s tendency toward irreverence can occasionally be economically inconvenient, but this tendency is also one of the major reasons for the paper's popularity.

Journalist Bites Reality! Steve Salerno. *Skeptic* (Altadena, Calif.). Skeptic v. 14 pp52–59 2008.

The fundamental flaws of broadcast journalism are so great, Salerno writes in this article, that its utility as a tool for informing viewers is almost zero. In its most basic form, the author writes, journalism deals with anomaly: it reports what life is not. Journalists over-react to events that fall within the realms of probability because they do not understand the difference between random data and genuine statistical inference, or they feel that the distinction hampers the dramatic impact and accessibility of the story, Salerno writes. When the broadcast media give prominence to marginal or meaningless events, they add legitimacy or relevance to those events, and this has an impact on how people see and live their lives, Salerno concludes.

Science Journalism in Free Fall. Robert Naeye. *Sky and Telescope* v. 118 p8 August 2009.

The writer bemoans the declining quality of science journalism, citing a number of per-sonal experiences that illustrate failures to verify facts, consult independent sources, or conduct original reporting. The changing ways in which people obtain science news and the expectation of instant and free information have led to a decline in quality that is un-likely to be recovered in the near future, if ever, Naeye writes. He adds that as science sec-tions disappear from daily newspapers for cost reasons, more and more people obtain sci-ence news from blogs and podcasts, which vary wildly in quality and often have an agenda, and this erosion of quality will have negative consequences for science and society.

Everyone's a Journalist. Joe Saltzman. *USA Today* (Periodical) v. 134 p59 November 2005.

Professional journalists need to accept that bloggers have every right to publish their views, Saltzman writes. There is so much talk about bloggers threatening professional journalists in the gathering and dissemination of news, he maintains, that the majority of people seem to forget that the notion of a "professional journalist'" is a product of the 20th century and not typical of the way journalism has been practiced throughout the centuries. Saltzman writes that the concept of freedom of the press asserts that everyone in a free and open society should have their own "press," enabling all people to voice their own view of the world and to report whatever is considered to be important. Professional journalists can also take comfort, the author says, from the fact that somebody always will be needed to uncover facts and put a story into perspective, and nobody does this better than the professional journalist.

Index

About the Editor

A proud son of the Constitution State, PAUL McCAFFREY was born in Danbury, Connecticut, and raised in Brookfield. He graduated from the Millbrook School and Vassar College in Duchess County, New York, and began his career with the H.W. Wilson Company in 2003 as a staff writer for *Current Biography*. In 2005 he became an assistant editor in the General Reference Department, working on The Reference Shelf series, and was promoted to editor in 2007. Among The Reference Shelf titles he has personally edited or coedited are *Hispanic Americans*, *The United States Supreme Court*, and *Global Climate Change*. He has also authored books for Chelsea House's Women of Achievement series, the first of which, *Ruth Bader Ginsburg*, is slated for publication in October 2010. He lives in Brooklyn, New York.